retro girl embroidery

retro girl embroidery

20 VINTAGE
PATTERNS INSPIRED BY
the 1970s

erin essiambre

FOUNDER OF SALT WATER STITCHES

PAGE STREET
PUBLISHING CO.

PAGE STREET
PUBLISHING CO.

First published in 2022 by
Page Street Publishing Co.
27 Congress Street, Suite 1511
Salem, MA 01970
www.pagestreetpublishing.com

Distributed by Macmillan, sales in Canada by The Canadian Manda Group.

26   25   24   23   22   1   2   3   4   5

ISBN-13: 978-1-64567-567-9
ISBN-10: 1-64567-567-X

Library of Congress Control Number: 2022932400

Cover and book design by Rosie Stewart for Page Street Publishing Co.
Photography by Erin Essiambre

Printed and bound in the United States

Dedicated to my grandma,

Margaret Pallos.

I hope you would be proud.

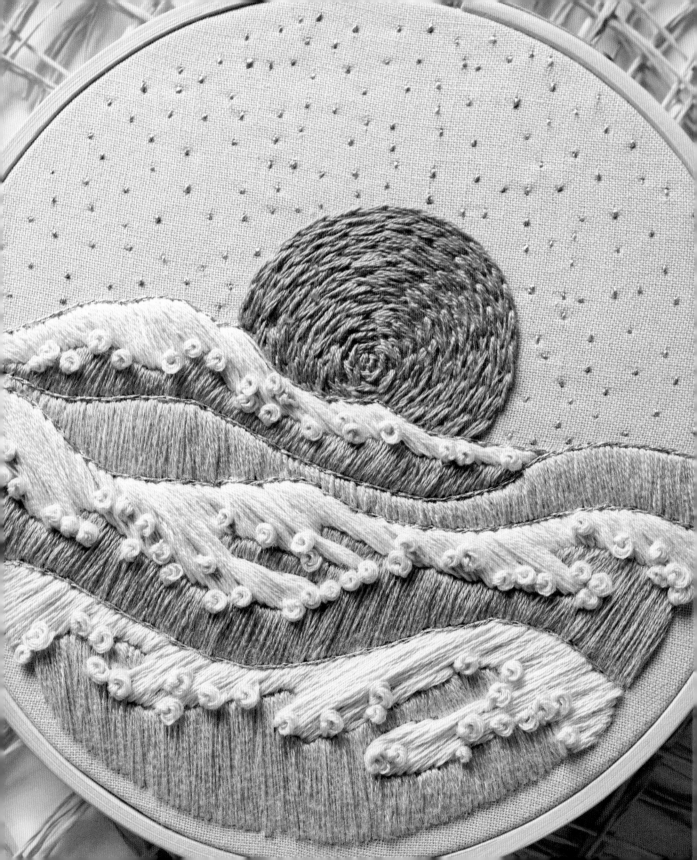

contents

introduction

I have always been a creative person. When we were growing up, my sister and I would host a pretend craft show at our kitchen table. We would ask my mom to save all the toilet paper rolls and then we would create something out of them that we were proud of, all while looking at an imaginary camera. It's funny how those days seem like they happened yesterday. Time is funny like that. When I look back at my life so far, in many ways I feel like I was created to create.

I'm going to be honest: Embroidery is one medium that I never saw myself gravitating toward. I've always loved to sketch, to doodle and draw. If you flipped through my high school notebooks, you would see the margins full of sketches of small faces, lots of little flowers and leaves, and sometimes the occasional random word handwritten ornately.

Flashing forward a few years, I always dreamed of being a mother. After being married at 21 years old, I especially felt that pull. I wanted nothing more than to raise a child, to be nurturing and loving. After having my son in 2018, I was ecstatic and overjoyed, yet I felt the pull to go back to creating. My soul was missing something; I needed to create to feel like myself again.

My sister had been dabbling in embroidery for a few months around this time, but ultimately, she felt that it wasn't for her. I was so intrigued by it, though; I couldn't stop staring at some of her creations. She offered to give me a few of her embroidery supplies since she wasn't into it anymore and I jumped at the opportunity!

I sat down one evening after putting my son to bed and began to stitch. I really didn't know what I was doing. I didn't know any official embroidery stitches or techniques, and I didn't even follow a pattern. I just sketched something quickly onto the fabric with a pencil I found on the kitchen counter and gave it a go. But with each stitch I pushed through the fabric, it was like someone was stitching my own soul back together. I stood back to look at my first creation and felt so much pride. I was officially in love with this art form.

Like I said, when I started embroidery, I didn't use a pattern because I couldn't find one that I felt fit my style and aesthetic. I began designing my own patterns and started an Instagram account, @SaltWaterStitches, so I could share my designs without feeling like I was "annoying" those on my personal account. I began to regularly share my new hoops and designs on Instagram, and slowly but surely I started to gain followers from all walks of life. What I found—much to my happiness—is that my patterns and story resonated with a lot of people. Here I am, almost three years later with thousands of followers who are the most supportive audience and community I could ask for. Creating art for a living is one thing, but to have it appreciated and cherished is something truly precious. My heart is full!

(continued)

My goal with this book is that you're able to find some time for yourself, that my designs speak to you and that you're able to create something for yourself that will give you some pride and joy when you stand back and look at it. These designs are a piece of my heart and soul, and I hope that you love stitching them and will cherish them forever—whether you are keeping the hoop for yourself or even gifting it to a friend. Perhaps some of these designs will even strike a chord of nostalgia within yourself!

When I think of these 20 designs, the word "nostalgia" truly does come to mind. The feeling of our warm childhood home while my mom played Fleetwood Mac on vinyl in the background. Creating crafts with my sister at the kitchen table while a storm rolled in; the smell of muffins being baked in the oven. Flipping through a photo album at my grandparents' house and looking at snapshots from the past, seeing the styles my mom and aunties used to wear. In an uncertain world, the feeling of familiarity is comforting. During the past two years, while navigating a global pandemic, there is nothing I wanted more than to revert to some of the most comforting times of my life.

My wish is that these retro patterns speak to you and comfort you. Each design purposely complements the next. I like to think that you will find multiple projects to stitch for yourself as you flip through this book. The theme, colors and textures of each hoop will only grow in beauty when they are placed next to each other and displayed in your home! These hoops will look amazing on a gallery wall, as a gift to a loved one or as a special project just for you. These patterns are warm and retro, with smooth edges and fluffy clouds. Something about flipping through these just feels like home. By reading through this book and stitching these designs, I invite you into my world and home, and I hope you're able to enjoy yourself and learn a few new tricks along the way.

getting started with embroidery

Embroidery is widely considered an older art form, but these days it has been modernized and taken to a whole different level. Embroidery definitely had a shining moment in the '70s. It was an era of self-expression, with colors, textures and patterns as bold as the opinions that people held! Embroidery helped to share those expressions through designs on clothing such as stitching on bell-bottom jeans or on the back of a jacket. When you think about it, has anything really changed in our era? Today, embroidery is used as a creative outlet and an artistic form of personal expression, whether by customizing clothing, putting a new spin on a vintage item or just boldly proclaiming a statement via embroidered lettering on clothing or a hoop. Every artist puts their own modern twist on their designs.

Embroidery can also relax and put the mind at ease. Personally, I love to stitch when my son is napping. I pour myself a cup of coffee, put on my favorite TV show or podcast and stitch away. It's a great way to relieve any stress by just focusing on the pattern in front of you.

Before you sit down to do the embroidering, there are a few things that you should know and supplies you need to gather. When I began embroidering, I figured out things on my own and was completely self-taught. It's my pleasure to go through the things I've personally learned with you now! These are a few of my favorite products and brands that I use on a daily basis, as well as my core stitches and techniques for getting started.

TOOLS AND MATERIALS

Hoops

The first thing you'll need when you are gathering supplies is a hoop. Hoops come in many different shapes, sizes and materials. There are wooden hoops, bamboo hoops and plastic hoops. You can buy them in circular or oval shapes, or even squares! Different types of hoops can be found at your local craft store such as Michaels®, in the craft section at discount stores like Walmart or on the web at the DMC® online store. My preferred type of hoop is made of bamboo. I find they are affordable and easy to source. When purchasing a bamboo or wooden hoop, be sure to look for imperfections such as lumps, any gaps between the outer and inner hoop or any splintering in the wood itself. The ideal hoop will be nice and tight and have no gaps. For the different patterns in this book, the instructions will specify which hoop size will suit the design best. However, if you would prefer not to purchase multiple sizes of hoops, a 9-inch (23-cm) hoop will fit every design in this book.

Fabric

Once you have found the perfect hoop, it's time to move on to choosing your fabric! Personally, I love to use 100% cotton for stitching. My favorite type of cotton to use is quilting cotton, or more specifically Kona® cotton. There are so many colors to choose from. The fabric stays nice and tight in the hoop, and I find the thread glides seamlessly through the fabric. Quilting cotton can be found in the quilting section at your local fabric store, or you can find it online. Online fabric shops, such as JOANN, Michaels and, in Canada, Piece Fabric Co., are my favorite places to buy fabric!

A tip for helping to keep the fabric tight in the hoop is to double-layer the fabric in the hoop. Instead of using only the one layer of fabric with the design on it, layer another piece of fabric cut to the same size under it. The double layer of fabric will help keep the hoop even tighter. Double-layering the fabric and maintaining that thickness is especially crucial for designs that feature my fluffy yarn clouds (page 24) or large portions of satin stitch. However, be sure to use the recommended needle size for each pattern so you won't struggle with pulling the thread or yarn through the layers of fabric.

Thread and Yarn

The main embroidery threads I use in every single design and throughout this book are by DMC. In every pattern you will find a number for the DMC thread color. I purchase all my DMC threads from my local Michaels store. They have a great selection there! I find DMC threads are very good quality and do not knot up like other brands do. Of course, you are welcome to use whatever threads you prefer to stitch the designs in this book—this is just what works best for me!

When you purchase the threads, cut off a small piece about the length of your thumb. Examine the thread and pull it apart. You will notice that the thread is composed of six smaller, singular strands. Each step of the designs in this book will let you know if the stitching calls for one strand, three strands or all six strands. By splitting the thread before stitching, you can really add in details to the design that wouldn't be possible if you were using all six strands constantly.

The next type of thread I use in most of my designs is metallic thread. I love to use DMC Diamant thread, specifically in the color Light Gold. This type of thread can be tricky to work with, but I promise that the end result is worth it! Diamant thread is a single-strand thread—no splitting of strands required. Its single-strand nature requires a little more patience. When looking in stores to purchase this thread, be sure to get the regular Diamant thread and not the Diamant Grande thread, as I find the Grande size much harder to work with.

When it comes to yarn, I like to use a thinner option such as Loops & Threads® Impeccable™ yarn or DMC Tapestry Wool. These yarns have a nice consistency and work well when being pulled through the fabric. Those two brands would be my first choice when embroidering with yarn! Thicker yarns can be used as well, such as Loops & Threads Charisma™ yarn, but will just take that extra little bit of effort to push it through the fabric. The final result is a nice, fluffy texture! When stitching with yarn, you do not pull apart the strands as you would with embroidery thread. Instead, you stitch with the full strand of yarn!

Needles

Now that we've talked about the thread, it's time to talk about needles! At the store, it can be a little overwhelming to try and decide which needles to buy. I like to use different sized needles depending on what I'm stitching.

If you're stitching a pattern, such as one in The Retro Girls chapter (page 29), completing a basic outline or stitching with metallic thread, I like to use a needle from the DMC Embroidery Needles pack in sizes 1–5. This is a good multitasker pack. These needles will help you complete most patterns and stitches such as back split stitch and French knots, and they are also great to use when stitching with DMC Diamant thread.

When a pattern calls for satin stitching, I like to switch to a needle from the DMC Darners Needle pack, sizes 1–5. This pack might be labeled for darning, but it is a great set of needles specifically for satin stitching because these needles will pull all six strands of thread through the fabric more easily than the embroidery needles.

The last needle type to mention is the type used when working with yarn. The type of needle I use to make my fluffy yarn clouds is the DMC Darners Needle pack, sizes 14–18. I use the largest size in the pack and find that this needle is easily able to pull the yarn through the fabric.

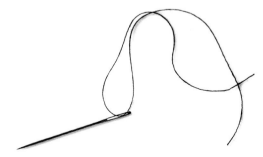

Threading the Needle

1. Begin by selecting the appropriate number of threads or yarn as listed in the pattern along with a needle that fits the number of threads you're using. The Stitch Guide and Special Techniques section (page 18) will tell you which needle is appropriate for the stitch you'll be completing. You may have to split the threads before threading the needle if the pattern calls for it.

2. Push the threads through the eye of the needle and then tie a small knot around the base of the needle.

3. Tie a small knot at the very end of the threads. This will ensure that your threads do not pull completely through the fabric!

TRANSFERRING THE DESIGNS TO FABRIC

Here you will find two of my favorite methods that you can use to transfer your design to fabric so it's ready to stitch.

The Transfer Paper Method

Begin by purchasing black carbon paper. I like to buy mine online in a pack of fifty sheets since I use mine up so quickly! You can also find these at a local office supply store. If you are transferring a design to darker fabric, you can find white transfer paper at Michaels under the brand name Craft Smart®.

First, take your fabric and lay it flat on the table. Make sure there are no bumps or bubbles in the fabric. Next, take your carbon paper and place it down over the

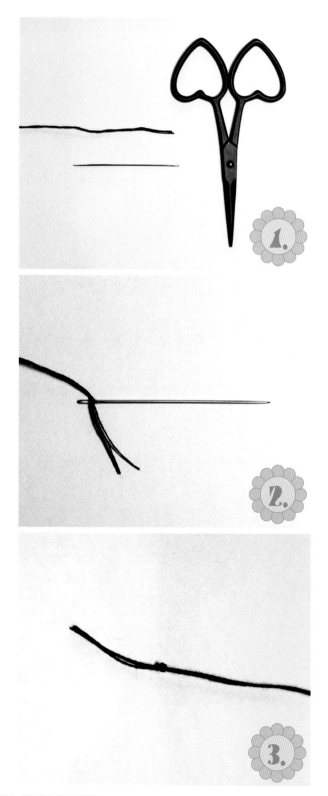

The Transfer Paper Method

top of the fabric so that the transfer side is touching the fabric. Now it's time to lay the pattern on top of the carbon paper. You can choose to trace the pattern directly from the book, or you can first photocopy the pattern out of the book and then trace the pattern. By tracing the design from a photocopy, you will be able to trace the same design multiple times over. Using a ballpoint pen, trace over the design. Be sure not to rest your arm or palm too firmly on the paper, as the pressure may transfer that spot to the fabric as well! Once you're done, gently peel away the pattern and the carbon paper. You will be left with your pattern on the fabric, ready to be put in the hoop.

Pros of the Transfer Paper Method: You will have an extremely crisp, clean transfer to the fabric because you can keep your hand steady while tracing the design. You can also reuse the pieces of carbon paper multiple times before moving on to a new sheet!

Cons of the Transfer Paper Method: Some people find the carbon paper a bit difficult to work with. The carbon paper lines are not erasable from the fabric, so you have to be sure to stitch over each line carefully.

The Lightbox Method

Using a source of light such as a window or lightbox, tape the pattern to the source of light. Then tape your pre-cut fabric on top of the pattern. The next step will be to take a heat-erasable pen, such as a Pilot® FriXion® pen, and trace the design onto the fabric. If you do not wish to purchase a heat-erasable pen, have no fear! Follow these same steps using a regular pencil. Please note that the lines will be slightly lighter with a pencil.

Once the pattern has been traced, you can gently remove the tape and the fabric from the window as well as the pattern. Gently peel the tape off both the pattern and fabric. Your fabric is now ready to put in the hoop and stitch!

Pros of the Lightbox Method: By using a heat-erasable pen to transfer the pattern, you're able to erase the lines after you're done stitching by using a blow-dryer on a low setting. This is great for someone new to embroidery! By using a pencil, the lines will be nice and light, and your stitches will cover over them with ease.

Cons of the Lightbox Method: Sometimes it can be hard to have a steady hand or find a light source bright enough to really see every detail of the pattern while transferring it. If using a pencil, once you've completed the stitching, the lines will be a bit harder to erase if you do not perfectly cover them with your stitches.

STITCH GUIDE AND SPECIAL TECHNIQUES

In this section, you will find all the embroidery stitches used in this book! Each type of stitch is listed, along with the directions on how to complete the stitch. I've also included some of my personal helpful tips. I hope you find this guide informative and easy to follow! Remember, practice makes perfect, so don't feel bad if you don't get the stitch perfect immediately! I promise you'll be a pro in no time. Please feel free to bookmark this page. I've created this section especially for you to be able to flip back and refer to when needed!

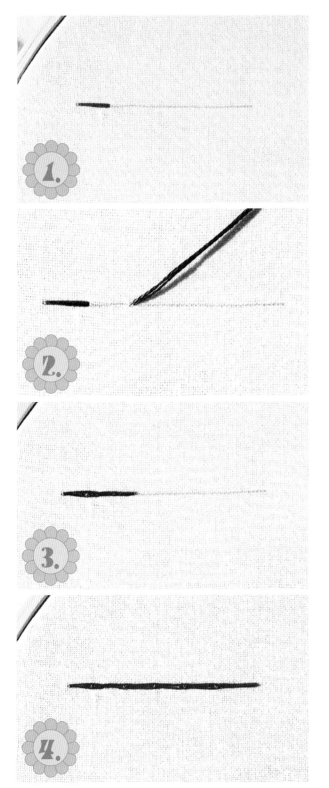

Stitches

BACK SPLIT STITCH

Back split stitch is the most often-used stitch in all of these designs. This stitch is great for outlining. When used for an outline, each stitch blends into the last one so that the eye isn't drawn to any gaps in the stitches of the outline. I also really like to use it for filling in shapes; this technique gives an incredible texture and shine to the embroidery thread that will have people asking what exactly you used to fill it in!

1. Begin by threading your needle. I like to pick the largest needle from the DMC Embroidery Needles pack sizes 1–5. These sit in the very middle of the pack. Push the needle through the backside of the fabric and stitch a straight line going forward. The length of the stitch should be about as long as your pinky nail.

2. Next, push your needle through the backside of the fabric. The gap between the first stitch and where you push the needle up should be the same length as the first stitch.

3. Push your needle down through the middle of the first original stitch, pushing it right through the thread itself.

4. Continue this same pattern until you have finished the line, continuously pushing the needle back through the center of the stitch before it.

GETTING STARTED WITH EMBROIDERY **19**

SATIN STITCH

Satin stitch is used to fill in a chunk of space or a shape. It is called satin stitch because when it's complete, the space you just filled in looks very satiny and smooth. Satin stitch can be completed by filling in the space using parallel lines, either vertically or horizontally.

Each pattern will vary in how many threads are required for the satin stitch portion of that design. Before threading your needle for stitching, it helps to split the threads. Do this by cutting off the desired portion of thread—about one arm's length. As previously mentioned, embroidery thread is composed of six smaller single strands. Split the thread into two groups of three strands. Once you have the two groups completely pulled apart, piece the two groups back together and then thread the needle as you would normally. Splitting the thread into two groups and then piecing it back together like this will help prevent any twisting of the thread when you are satin stitching! The thread will lay a lot flatter and smoother against the fabric.

1. Begin by threading the needle. I like to use a needle from the DMC Darners Needle pack sizes 1–5. Push the needle through the underside of the fabric, and then back down on the other side of your shape. Always push the needle up through the fabric on the same side as where you started and push it down through the fabric on the opposite side.

2. Take your time building up the stitches one after another, each stitch sitting parallel to the last one. Gradually, your shape will start to fill in. The end result is a nice chunk of satin stitch that looks seamlessly filled in!

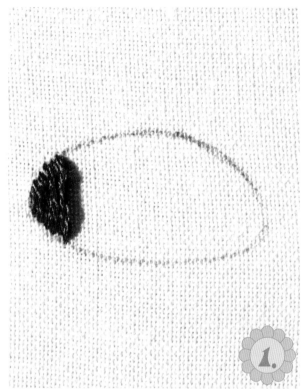

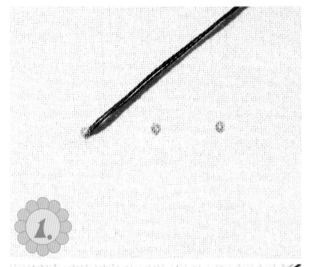

FRENCH KNOT

French knots are a beautiful way to add some texture and dimension to a design! I mainly use French knots to fill in the cloud shapes on my designs. Because French knots have a fluffy texture, they are great for clouds or anything that you want to make look "soft"! A classic French knot wraps the thread around the needle twice, but for my French knots I always wrap the thread around the needle three times.

1. Begin by threading the needle. I always choose a needle from the DMC Embroidery Needles pack sizes 1–5. Push the needle up through the underside of the fabric.

2. With the tip of your needle gently pressed against the fabric, wrap the long thread around the needle three times, using medium tension.

3. Begin to push the needle back down through the fabric, just a tiny bit away from where the needle was originally pushed up through the fabric. As you're pushing down and pulling the thread through, hold the longer piece of thread with your hand, keeping the tension of the thread.

RUNNING STITCH

A running stitch is one of the most basic embroidery stitches. This stitch can have many uses, including cinching the back of a hoop or adding some tiny specks of stars to a design. Two patterns that use running stitch to create a star effect are Ocean at Sunset (page 79) and Moon Garden (page 99)!

1. Start by threading an embroidery needle with your thread of choice and knotting the end of the thread. Push the needle up from the underside of the fabric. Push the needle down ¼ inch (6 mm) away from where you pushed the needle up. The stitch should be about the length of a grain of rice.

2. Continue the same process as step 1 until you have completed a line. The distance between each stitch should be about ⅛ inch (3 mm) or about half the size of the stitch before it.

things to note: *When using the running stitch to fill in a starry sky, try to be less precise with the measurement of the stitches. I try to make them smaller than a grain of rice. You want them to really resemble tiny little specks of stars. Having these little stitches vary in size will give more of a random star-like look that will truly mimic the night sky. Do not focus on perfection—the more imperfect the little stitches look, the more realistic the sky will look!*

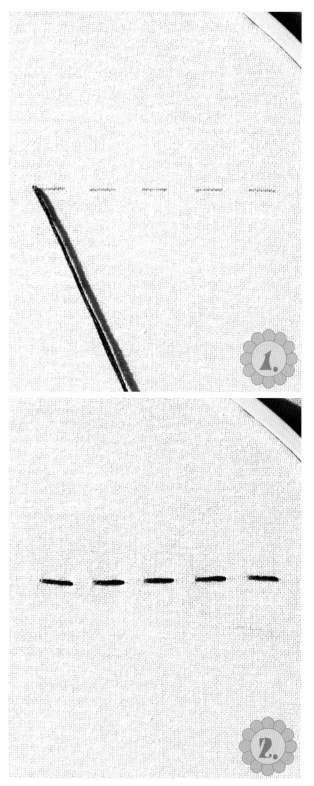

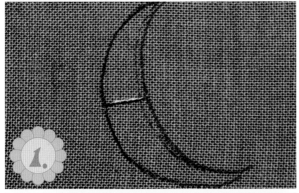

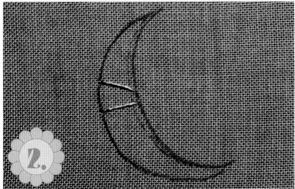

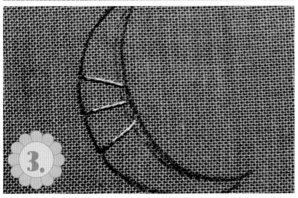

MOON TECHNIQUE

There is nothing I love more than a nice, shiny metallic moon added into my designs! It really has become one of the signature traits in my patterns. Here I will show you how I fill in my moons. It is a form of satin stitch, but at a gradual angle, which I explain more below!

1. Begin by threading your needle. I like to use a needle from the DMC Embroidery Needles pack in sizes 1–5. Begin by pushing the needle up through the fabric on the center of the right side of the moon, then push the needle down through the center of the left side of the moon.

2. Push the needle up through the fabric on the right side of the moon, slightly above where the original line is, and then angle the thread about 45 degrees up and to the left and push it through the fabric. The goal is to keep stitching at angles following the curve of the moon.

3. Push the needle up through the fabric, slightly below the right side of the first original stitch. Angle the thread about 45 degrees down and to the left.

4. Follow this curve using satin stitch to fill in the moon. Having those initial three stitches as a guide will make it easier to follow that curve of the moon.

FLUFFY CLOUD TECHNIQUE

My fluffy yarn clouds are one of my most beloved techniques. Since I started creating my cloud hoops, I've received hundreds of comments and messages asking exactly what my secret is and how I bring the whimsical clouds to life. I've never shared my secrets before, but I'm about to now!

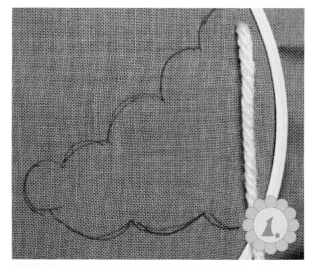

The steps you'll be following are extremely similar to completing a French knot, but with a few extra steps added in to really layer on the fluffiness. Try to give the yarn a bit of tension while completing the French knots, but keep it fairly loose as you stitch. Keeping them loose is what will give it that fluffy texture. The more you layer the French knots on top of each other, the better the illusion of a real cloud!

1. Start by threading yarn through the size 18 darning needle from the DMC Darners Needle pack sizes 14–18. I like to use a lightweight yarn such as DMC Tapestry Wool or Loops & Threads Impeccable yarn. I like to start on the edge of the cloud. Push the needle up through the fabric.

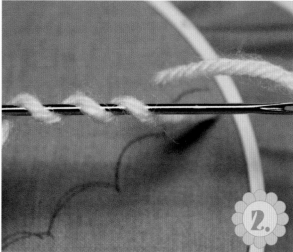

2. With your needle gently hovering above the fabric, wrap the long yarn around the needle three times, using medium tension.

3. Begin to push the needle back down through the fabric, just a tiny way away from where the needle was originally pushed up through the fabric. As you're pushing down and pulling the yarn through, hold the longer piece of yarn with your hand, keeping the tension of the yarn.

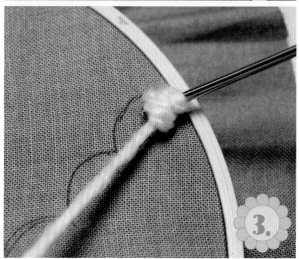

4. Follow this same process along the edge of the cloud, with the French knots sitting side by side. Occasionally, when pushing the needle down through the fabric, push it down through the side of the French knot beside it. This will help to layer the French knots on top of each other and really build that volume. It will also help to not show any gaps between the French knots.

5. Work your way into the center of the cloud still using the French knot method. Occasionally, instead of wrapping the yarn around the needle three times, wrap it four or five times! Switching up the number of wraps will really create that realistic cloud look and add varying volume.

6. Once the cloud is filled in, push the needle up through the fabric and begin to pin the knots together by pushing the needle back down through random French knots. Make sure the tension is a bit looser to create little "bubbles" of yarn. Again, this will add more texture and fluffiness. Focus the volume and height of the cloud more in the center, making sure that the cloud doesn't look super perfect! It should look a little irregular, which will make it look more realistic.

STAR TECHNIQUE

Having at least a few stars in my designs is pretty common! I just love the twinkle and retro feel that they give a pattern. I have a certain way that I like to stitch them, which I detail below.

1. Start by threading your needle. I always choose a needle from the DMC Embroidery Needles pack in sizes 1–5. Push the needle up through the fabric on the middle-right point of the star, then push the needle down through the middle-left point of the star.

2. Push the needle up through the bottom-middle point of the star and down through the top-middle point of the star.

3. Next, fill in the star using satin stitch in vertical lines on either side of the longest vertical strand you just stitched.

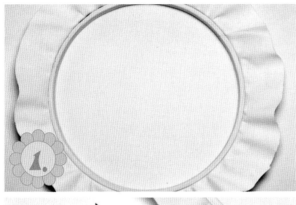

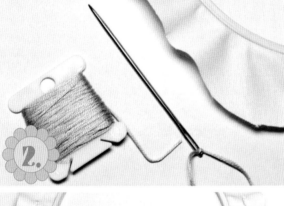

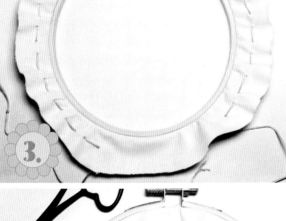

FINISHING THE HOOP

Okay, so now you've stitched your design beautifully. Yay! You've stood back and admired your work . . . but now what? How do you finish the back and make it ready to display on the wall or gift to a loved one? Not to worry! Follow the steps below for a simple way to finish the back of the hoop.

Cinching the Back of the Hoop

1. Trim the fabric around the edge of the hoop so that there's about an inch (2.5 cm) of fabric from the edge of the hoop to the outer edge of the fabric.

2. Thread your needle (choose the size 18 needle, which is the largest size needle from the DMC Darners Needle pack sizes 14–18) with all 6 strands of the embroidery thread of your choice. I like to choose a thread color that is similar to the color of the fabric.

3. Using a running stitch (page 22), slowly stitch along the middle of the fabric until you've reached your starting point.

4. Take your needle off the thread and grab both ends of the thread. Pull the ends of the threads tight and tie two knots. This will cinch the fabric.

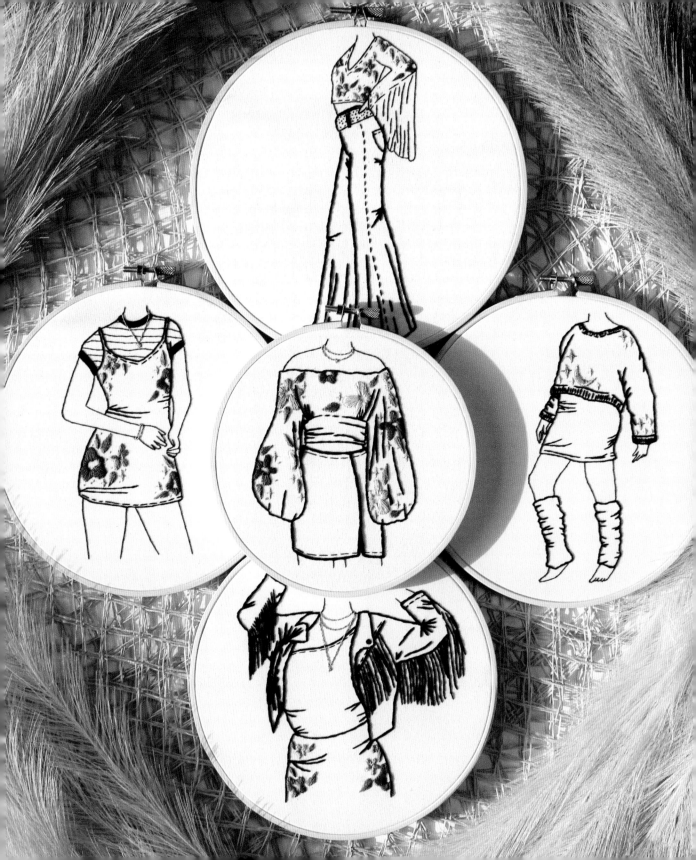

the retro girls

Having a chapter, let alone an entire book, based on my Retro Girl designs is truly a pinch-me moment. Before I created my first Retro Girl, I was still a newer artist, struggling to find my own creative voice in a world of other talented embroidery artists. One day I was browsing through pictures of fashions from the '70s and a collective wash of "wow" ran over me. I couldn't stop thinking about how amazing an ode to the fashion of the '70s would be on an embroidery hoop. I sat down and sketched my very first one, which I aptly named "Retro Girl." She was the first, and although she had no real name of her own, she forever changed the face of my little business. I began to lean into the warmth and comfort provided by the colors and tones of the '70s. My Instagram feed changed from cold, bright tones to warm, sunlit photos of my work accompanied by retro fonts and music. I felt like I was truly becoming who I was meant to be as an artist.

Since that very first Retro Girl hoop, I've created multiple designs with that same style and feel. These girls are no exception! These Retro Girls are some of my absolute favorites that I've ever created. If I had to pick just one, I would have to say Hazel (page 47). I love the way her flowy shirt truly captures your attention, with the warm pops of color reaching out to you. I hope you enjoy stitching these designs. As you complete them, I hope they will bring life and movement to your walls and home, just as they did for me and my small business.

mia

I imagine that Mia spends her time thrift shopping on the weekends. She loves to blast a vinyl on her record player that was passed down to her from her parents. She also loves to mix and match her outfits, giving her that cool girl vibe! Of course, her gold jewelry ties the whole outfit together. This hoop is a perfect addition to the Retro Girl series, and I hope you love stitching her.

SUPPLIES NEEDED

White quilting cotton fabric

1 (7-inch [18-cm]) embroidery hoop

1 embroidery needle

DMC Thread colors: #310, #920, #3778, #831, #3820, DMC Diamant thread in Light Gold

#310 #920 #3778 #831 #3820

DMC Diamant thread in Light Gold

1. Begin by transferring the design on page 35 to your fabric using your preferred method (page 16) and placing the fabric in the hoop. We're going to begin by stitching the outline and creases of Mia's dress. Use 2 strands of #310 and back split stitch (page 19) to complete this.

2. Next, stitch her T-shirt. Use 2 strands of #310 and back split stitch to complete the outer shape of the T-shirt. When stitching the collar and sleeves, stitch in little vertical lines using satin stitch (page 20) to fill in the bulk of the shape. Once this is done, use 1 strand of #310 and back split stitch to outline the edges of the collar and sleeves. This will give it a crisper, cleaner look!

3. For the thin, horizontal lines on the T-shirt, use 1 strand of #310 and back split stitch. Do not worry about making these appear super straight or clean! Giving them a bit of a rougher texture will add a little visual interest.

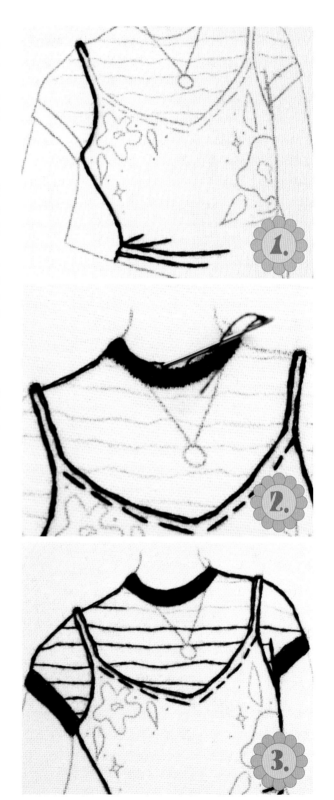

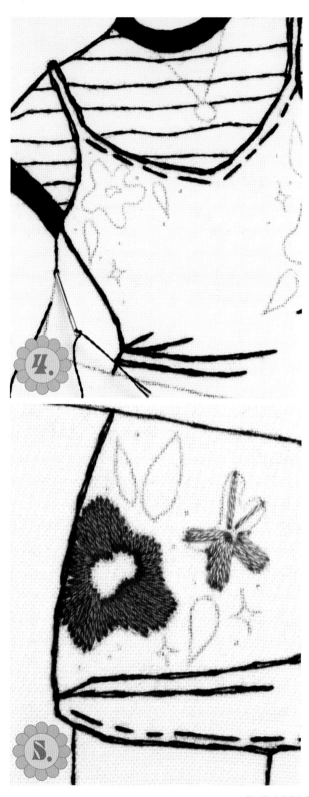

4. Now let's stitch the neck, arms and legs. To do this, use 1 strand of #310 and back split stitch. Using 1 strand will give the outline a more delicate look.

5. Since all the black outlining is now complete, we can focus on the fun pops of color! To fill in the flowers, we are going to use satin stitch. Use 3 strands of #920 for the more rounded flowers and 3 strands of #3778 for the flowers with five petals. When satin stitching the flowers, work clockwise, starting at the center of the flower.

(continued)

MIA (CONTINUED)

6. Now that the flowers have been filled in, it's time to stitch the leaves. Use 2 strands of #831 and satin stitch to fill them in.

7. The final details to add are the stars on her dress and the jewelry. These finishing touches will really bring the whole hoop together! For the stars on the dress, we are going to use 2 strands of #3820 and satin stitch (see page 26 for my Star Technique). For the jewelry, use DMC Diamant thread in Light Gold. When stitching the bracelets and necklace chain, use back split stitch. When filling in the necklace pendant, use satin stitch. Close off the hoop according to the directions on page 27.

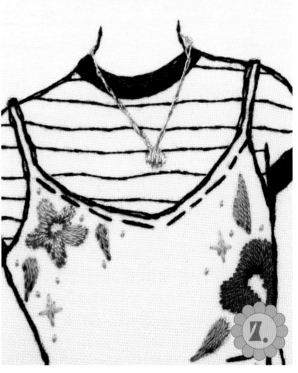

farrah

When I think of retro, I really think of bell-bottom or flare pants. They are so much fun and, dare I say, even a little flirty! I needed to design a girl wearing some classic flare pants and so Farrah was born. The pants combined with the draped arms on the shirt create a lot of movement in the design. Farrah is stitched on an 8-inch (20-cm) circular hoop but would also look amazing in an oval-shaped hoop to showcase her flare pants!

SUPPLIES NEEDED

White quilting cotton fabric

1 (8-inch [20-cm]) embroidery hoop

1 embroidery needle

DMC Thread colors: #310, #781, #920, #3778, #831, DMC Diamant thread in Light Gold

#310   #781   #920   #3778   #831

DMC Diamant thread in Light Gold

1. Begin by transferring the design on page 40 to your fabric using your preferred method (page 16) and placing the fabric in the hoop. Let's begin by stitching her pants! Do not stitch the seams down the side of the pants quite yet, though. To stitch the main outline of the pants, use 4 strands of #310 and back split stitch (page 19). Using 4 strands of thread gives the illusion of thicker fabric on the pants. When stitching the back pocket and the seam down the side of the pants, switch to using 2 strands of #310 and back split stitch.

2. Next, let's stitch her shirt. Use 1 strand of #310 and back split stitch. This will give a more delicate look and add dimension and flow to the shirt! Also use 1 strand of #310 and back split stitch to stitch her neck, stomach and thumb.

3. Now we'll stitch the belt and the belt loop. Use 2 strands of #310 and back split stitch to outline the belt. When stitching the tiny dots on the belt, switch to a running stitch (page 22) while still using 2 strands of #310.

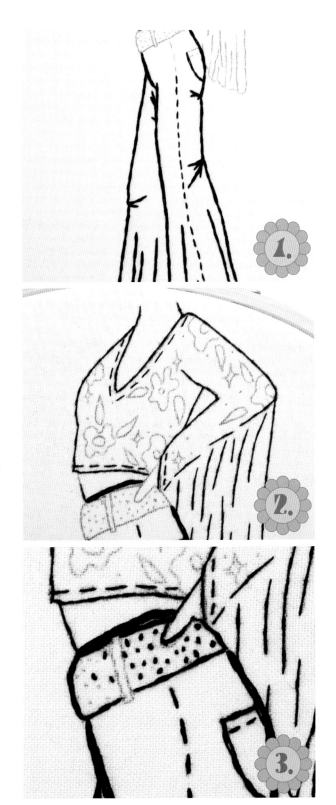

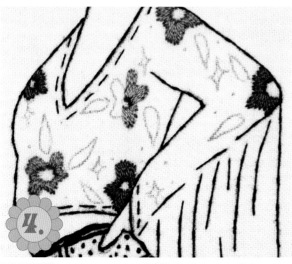

4. It's now time to stitch the flowers on the shirt using satin stitch (page 20) and 2 strands of thread. Be sure to stitch in a clockwise direction around the center of the flower. For the flowers, we are going to use three different colors: #781 for the flower on the bottom left of her shirt and the top of her shoulder; #920 for the top left of her shirt, the bottom right and the elbow; and #3778 for the last remaining flower.

5. Next, let's stitch the leaves and add in the greenery. To do this, use 2 strands of #831 and satin stitch.

6. Lastly, let's add in some gold detailing by completing the stars on her shirt. Use satin stitch and DMC Diamant thread in Light Gold (see page 26 for my Star Technique). Close off the back of the hoop according to the directions on page 27.

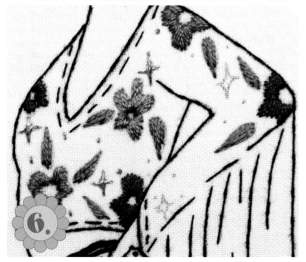

Sara

The inspiration for Sara came from watching too many '80s movies (if there is such a thing!) and being envious of the outfits worn in them. I love a good sweater or a cozy outfit, so I had to make a Retro Girl with a cozy athleisure feel! Although the '70s isn't known specifically for the leg warmer style, as exercise videos made their debut, so did the fad of leg warmers. I love that the details are subtle on the sweater, so the focus is on the outfit itself. Back split stitch is key for this design; this is a good pattern with which to really perfect your outlining skills!

SUPPLIES NEEDED

White quilting cotton fabric

1 (7-inch [18-cm]) embroidery hoop

1 embroidery needle

DMC Thread colors: #310, DMC Diamant thread in Light Gold, #976, #353

#310   #976   #353

DMC Diamant thread in Light Gold

1. Begin by transferring the design on page 45 to your fabric using your preferred method (page 16) and placing the fabric in the hoop. We are going to start by using 3 strands of #310 and back split stitch (page 19) to outline her sweater. Outline all parts of the sweater, including the neckline and cuffs. When it comes to stitching the cuffs and details in the sweater hem, make your stitches a tad smaller, about half the size of a grain of rice, while using back split stitch. By focusing on smaller stitch sizes, you will be able to follow the curve of the cuffs more closely. This will add such a nice depth of detail!

2. Now let's stitch her leg warmers! Again, use 3 strands of #310 and back split stitch.

3. Next, we are going to use 2 strands of #310 to outline her skirt. Use back split stitch to outline this.

(continued)

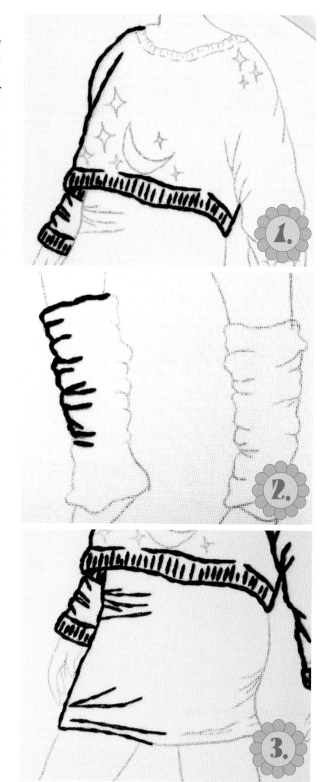

SARA (CONTINUED)

4. To stitch her neck, hands, legs and feet, we are going to use 1 strand of #310. Using 1 strand gives that more delicate outline. In contrast with the sweater and skirt, it provides that skin-like look!

5. Finally, let's add in the star and moon detailing! For the moon, we are going to use DMC Diamant thread in Light Gold. We are going to use satin stitch (page 20) for this (see page 23 for more on my Moon Technique). For the stars, use 2 strands of #976 for the larger stars and 2 strands of #353 for the smaller stars. Use satin stitch for the stars as well (see page 26 for my Star Technique). Feel free to switch up the colors of the moon and stars to whatever colors suit your taste! This is a great way to display your style and personality! Once these are complete, you will be done! Close off the back of the hoop according to the directions on page 27.

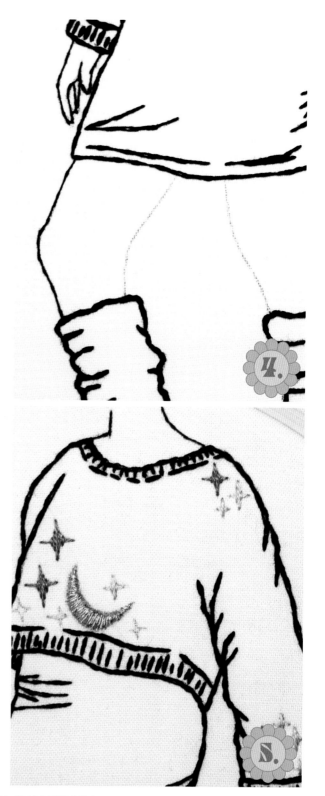

hazel

Hazel's shirt truly has my heart. The flowy nature of it, the embroidered chunky flowers— how can you not love it? This is an outfit that I would love to wear! I would say this is a definite must-stitch. Stitching the larger flowers on the shirt will really help you finesse your stitching skills when it comes to the retro florals in my designs. The flowy nature of her shirt, combined with the structure of her skirt, really ties all of the Retro Girls together. I can't imagine the series without her!

SUPPLIES NEEDED

White quilting cotton fabric

1 (6-inch [15-cm]) embroidery hoop

1 embroidery needle

DMC Thread colors: #310, #920, #353, #977, #781, #3852, DMC Diamant thread in Light Gold

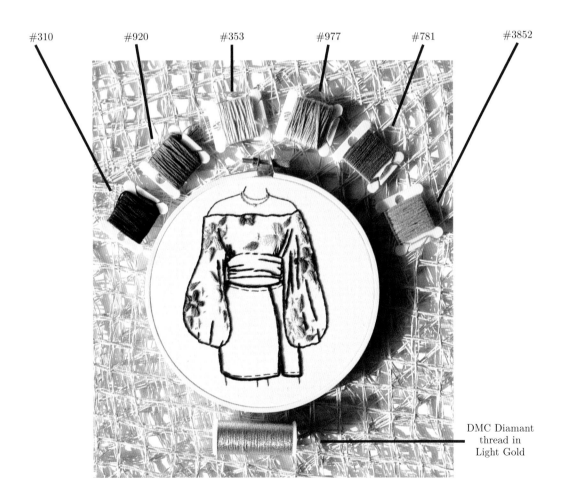

#310   #920   #353   #977   #781   #3852

DMC Diamant thread in Light Gold

1. Start by transferring your design on page 51 to the fabric using your preferred method (page 16) and placing the fabric in the hoop. Then begin the pattern by stitching Hazel's flowy shirt. Using 3 strands of #310 and back split stitch (page 19), start outlining the shirt as well as all its flowy creases.

2. Next, let's outline her skirt. Use all 6 strands of #310 and back split stitch to do this. Be sure to outline the main shape of the skirt as well as the line going down the middle of it.

3. Now we will focus on stitching the more delicate lines on the hoop. This includes her shoulders and neck, the sides of her stomach and her legs, as well as the little stitches on her skirt. To stitch all these parts, use 1 strand of #310 and back split stitch.

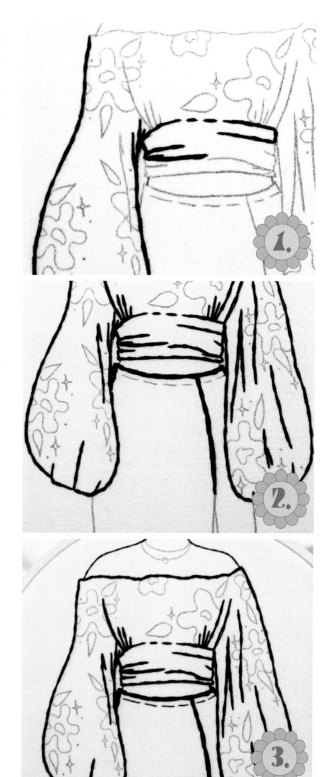

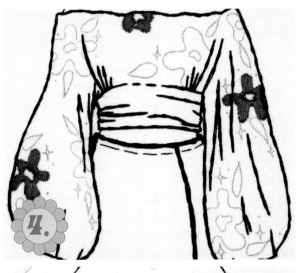

4. Let's fill in the pops of color on her shirt now! We'll start by focusing on the flowers. For all of the flowers in her shirt, we are going to use 3 strands of thread, satin stitch (page 20) and stitch in a clockwise motion around the center of each flower. Let's begin! Use #920 for the flower on the bottom of the left sleeve, the top of the middle neckline and the middle of the right sleeve.

5. Use #353 for the flower on the middle of the left sleeve, the right side of the chest area and the bottom of the right sleeve.

6. Use #977 for the flower on the top of the left sleeve and the very top of the right sleeve.

(continued)

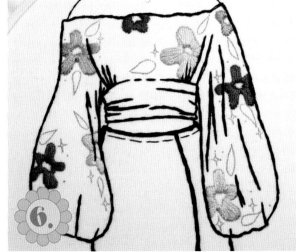

HAZEL (CONTINUED)

7. Use 3 strands of #781 and satin stitch for the leaves surrounding the flowers.

8. Use 1 strand of #3852 for the stars and the tiny dots. Use satin stitch for the stars (see page 26 for my Star Technique) and French knots (page 21) for the dots.

9. Finally, let's stitch the golden details. Using DMC Diamant thread in Light Gold and back split stitch, outline her necklace. For the tiny pendant on the necklace, use satin stitch. Close off the back of the hoop according to the directions on page 27.

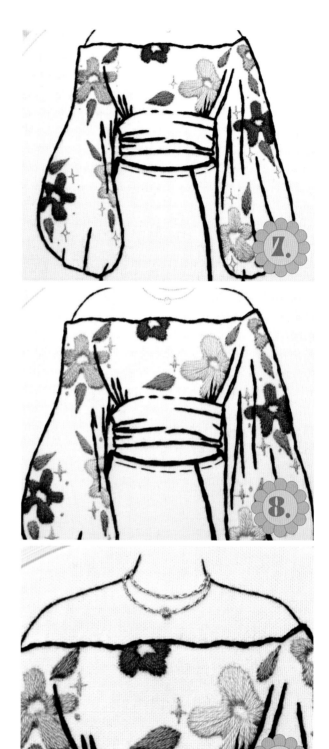

hazel template

jolene

Jolene's jacket is truly a showstopper. I feel like this fringe jacket is the epitome of retro and I just love how it ties in with the other Retro Girls. I can visualize her dancing around to music, waving her arms in the air with the fringe bouncing and swaying. This is another great design to practice back split stitch since outlining each fringe piece will require some patience. The result is worth it though—you'll have this cool girl to hang on your wall once you're done stitching!

SUPPLIES NEEDED

White quilting cotton fabric

1 (7-inch [18-cm]) embroidery hoop

1 embroidery needle

DMC Thread colors: #310, #831, #781, #920, #758, DMC Diamant thread in Light Gold

#310   #831   #781   #920   #758

DMC Diamant thread in Light Gold

1. Begin by transferring the design on page 57 to your fabric using your preferred method (page 16) and placing the fabric in the hoop. Our first step is to stitch her amazing, show-stopping jacket. For this, use 4 strands of #310 and back split stitch (page 19). Begin by stitching the arms and the main outline of the jacket as well as the creases.

2. Next, let's stitch all the fun fringe strips and little stitches on the jacket! To do this, use 2 strands of #310 and back split stitch.

3. To complete the jacket, let's add in the little button on the collar. Use 2 strands of #310 and satin stitch (page 20). Stitch in little vertical lines.

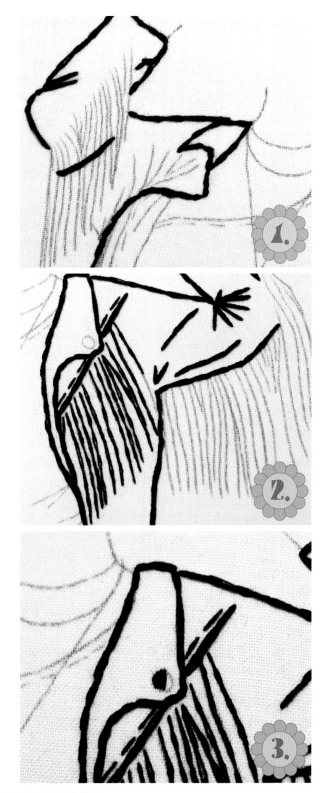

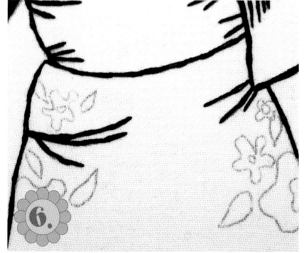

4. Now, let's move on to the arms and neck. Use 1 strand of #310 and back split stitch to complete this. Using a single strand will give the skin a nice delicate look.

5. Let's stitch her off-the-shoulder shirt. Use 3 strands of #310 and back split stitch for the outline. To stitch the small stitching detail on the shirt, use 1 strand of #310 and back split stitch. This dainty stitching will add a nice contrast to the outline of the shirt.

6. Finally, let's stitch her skirt! Use 3 strands of #310 and back split stitch to outline the main shape and creases in the skirt.

(continued)

JOLENE (CONTINUED)

7. Now comes the fun part! It's time to fill in the pops of color on her skirt. This will add even more visual interest to the hoop. Use 3 strands of #831 and satin stitch (page 20) to fill in the little leaves on the skirt.

8. For the flowers, we will be using satin stitch to complete all of them. Use 3 strands of #781 for the flower with the more rounded petals on the left side of the skirt, as well as the flower on the top right. Use 3 strands of #920 for the larger flower on the bottom right of the skirt. Use 3 strands of #758 to stitch both the flowers that have five petals. Stitch in a clockwise direction for each, working around the center of each flower.

9. Lastly, let's add in the gold jewelry! Use DMC Diamant thread in Light Gold and back split stitch to stitch each of the chains. Use satin stitch to add in the tiny little pendant on the chain. Close off the back of the hoop according to the directions on page 27.

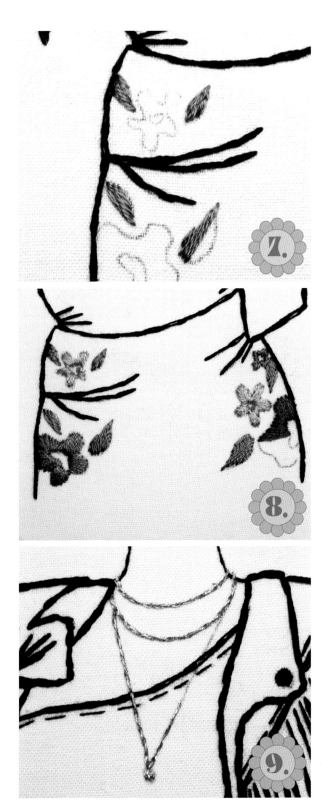

jolene template

whimsical & celestial

The night sky; who isn't inspired when they look up at the moon and millions of tiny stars? Originally, the idea for a starry night design came to me when I was creating embroidered pendants. I had just learned the art of stitching French knots and it popped into my brain that the stitch would lend itself beautifully to clouds! Well, I decided to try this same technique using a hoop and some yarn. Combine this with my love for metallic thread, and the Starry Night hoop (page 61) was born. Since then, thousands of people have loved this design on Instagram and have asked about my secrets on how I make this eye-catching design. I've never explained fully in a step-by-step format how I create these hoops, but it only feels right to share it all with you now!

Along with the classic Starry Night design, I have a few other show-stopping pieces such as the classic but easy Monochrome Sky design (page 71). There's also the beautiful and a bit more challenging Ocean at Sunset hoop (page 79). Whichever design you choose to stitch from this chapter, once finished, it is sure to be a timeless piece that will add that whimsical touch to any space. These designs are best stitched while listening to "Space Oddity" by David Bowie, which was released at the end of 1969, just as the '70s were being ushered in. Whether you press play on that particular song or choose a classic '70s playlist, the music will truly transport you back in time and fill your space with a celestial vibe!

starry night

This hoop is one of my Instagram followers' very favorites. I love the night sky, and one day I started to experiment with my own version using yarn on black fabric. The two lush clouds combined with the gold thread contrasting against the dark fabric is just so captivating. This piece would be amazing for a nursery, a bedroom or office wall—okay, really anywhere! When stitching this design, you may find that pulling the yarn through the fabric is a tad challenging at times, but have patience! If you're finding it really difficult, it may be best to stitch this hoop over a few sessions or switch to a lighter-weight yarn (I've included an alternative to the right). Enjoy stitching this iconic Salt Water Stitches design and have fun with it!

SUPPLIES NEEDED

Black quilting cotton fabric

1 (6-inch [15-cm]) embroidery hoop

1 embroidery needle

DMC Thread color: DMC Diamant thread in Light Gold

1 size 18 darner needle from the DMC Darners Needle pack sizes 14–18

Loops & Threads Charisma yarn in Off White (Alternatively, use Loops & Threads Impeccable yarn in the shade Aran. It is thinner and easier to pull through the fabric!)

Loops & Threads Charisma yarn in Off White

DMC Diamant thread in Light Gold

1. Transfer your design on to the fabric using your preferred method (page 16) and then place the fabric in the hoop. Begin to stitch the stars and moon using your embroidery needle and DMC Diamant thread in Light Gold. Use satin stitch (page 20) for the moon and the stars (see pages 23 and 26 for more on my Moon and Star Techniques). These gold details are truly what make the design pop off the fabric!

2. The next step will be to fill in the clouds. To do this, use the size 18 darning needle and Loops & Threads Charisma yarn in Off White. Use French knots (page 21) to give the illusion of fluffy clouds (read more about my Fluffy Cloud Technique on page 24). The large darning needle will make holes large enough to pull the yarn through the fabric. Once you are done stitching, close the back of the hoop according to the directions on page 27.

starry night template

desert at dusk

The desert is one of the most beautiful places. This design is heavily inspired by the Palm Desert, where we love to spend family time in the winter. When I sit down and stitch this piece, I automatically want to play "Hotel California" by the Eagles. This design gives me California desert in the '70s vibes. I just love the vibrant warm tones and gold stars. Can you imagine one of the Retro Girls walking on the side of the road, her fringe jacket bouncing, making her way to a music festival? The simple palm tree leaf on the left adds even more whimsy and magic to this design. Hanging this piece on your wall will give you a little bit of warmth and sunshine whenever you need it most!

SUPPLIES NEEDED

Quilting cotton in a robin's egg blue, such as Kona fabric in Blue

1 (6-inch [15-cm]) embroidery hoop

1 darner needle from the DMC Darners Needle pack sizes 1–5

DMC Thread colors: #920, #3830, #3778, #3823, #831, DMC Diamant thread in Light Gold

#831   #3823   #920   #3830   #3778

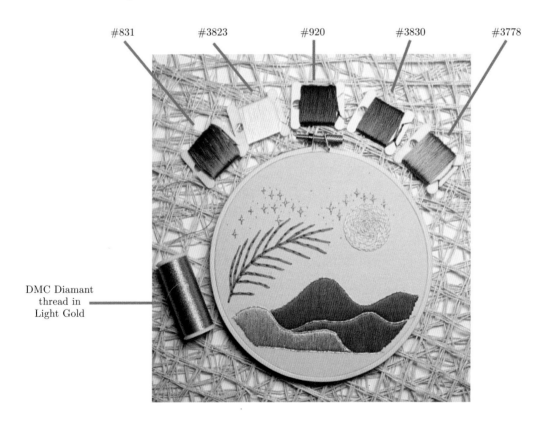

DMC Diamant thread in Light Gold

1. Transfer your design on page 69 to the fabric using your preferred method (page 16) and then place the fabric in the hoop. Now we are ready to begin stitching. Let's begin by using satin stitch (page 20) in vertical lines and 6 strands of #920 to stitch the top layer of the mountain.

2. Stitch the middle layer of the mountain using 6 strands of #3830 and satin stitch, using vertical lines again.

3. Lastly, the bottom layer of the mountain will be stitched using 6 strands of #3778 and satin stitch in vertical lines again.

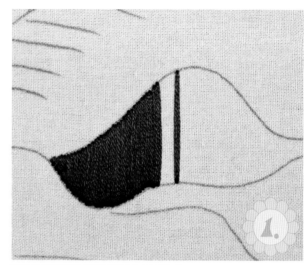

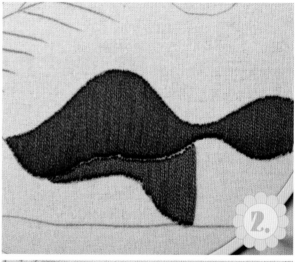

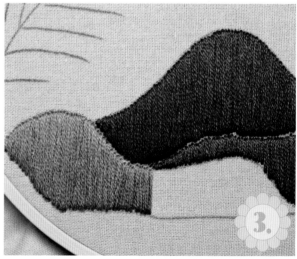

4. The next step will be to stitch the full moon. Using 6 strands of #3823 and back split stitch (page 19), start by stitching the outer circle shape of the moon. Create a slightly smaller circle using the same stitch on the inside of the circle you just made. Repeat this same process until you have filled the moon in completely. The moon should look like a large spiral once you're complete.

5. Next, we are going to stitch the palm tree branch. Do this using 6 strands of #831 and back split stitch. Start at the base of the main branch, working your way up to the tip. Once that is stitched, work on each individual leaf, working your way back down to the bottom leaves.

(continued)

6. Now let's move on to adding the gold detailing. Start by using DMC Diamant thread in Light Gold to stitch the stars in the sky (see page 26 for my Star Technique). Use satin stitch for these. When it comes to the little dots, use a running stitch (page 22) to add tiny little specks of stars.

7. Let's outline the edges of the mountains using DMC Diamant thread in Light Gold. Use a back split stitch for this. Start at the top of the first layer of mountain, working your way through the middle and the bottom mountain layers. Next, outline the straight line at the very bottom base of the mountains. Lastly, finish the back of your hoop according to the directions on page 27.

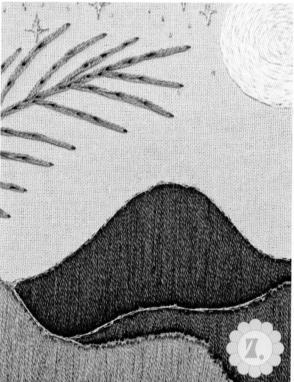

monochrome sky

Monochrome designs are so refreshing. There's just something about being drawn into the design itself without any of the noise that colors usually add! Because of the calming nature of this piece, I feel like it would be the perfect addition to a nursery or bedroom. This piece uses yarn, so it's a great design to practice using the large darning needle!

SUPPLIES NEEDED

Cream or white quilting cotton fabric

1 (6-inch [15-cm]) embroidery hoop

Loops & Threads Impeccable yarn in Aran

1 size 18 darner needle from the DMC Darners Needle pack sizes 14–18

Loops & Threads Impeccable yarn in Aran

1. Transfer the design to your fabric using your preferred method (page 16) and place the fabric in the hoop. Take the roll of Loops & Threads Impeccable yarn and cut off an arm's length. Thread the yarn through a size 18 darning needle and begin to fill in the moon using my Moon Technique (read more on page 23). Once this is complete, begin to fill in the dots and stars. Use a running stitch (page 22) for the dots. The stars are smaller and will not look as detailed as they would with embroidery thread—but that's okay! It gives the piece a nice chunky look. The larger stars should resemble a lower case "t" (see page 26 for more on my Star Technique).

2. Next, using the same yarn and darning needle, we are going to fill in the clouds! Using French knots (page 21) and the Fluffy Cloud Technique (page 24), fill them in. Once this is done, you'll be ready to finish the back of the hoop according to the directions on page 27.

warm desert

The colors and textures featured in this design are truly something special! The movement of the rolling hills and the fluffy clouds play off each other so nicely. This design would be a great addition to a gallery wall, office space or anywhere you want to daydream a little every now and then!

#3826   #3778   #729   #781   #3771

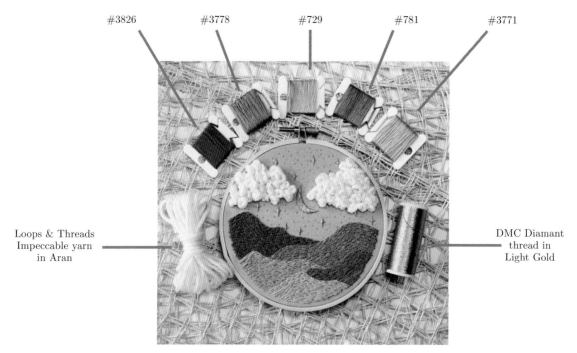

Loops & Threads
Impeccable yarn
in Aran

DMC Diamant
thread in
Light Gold

1. Begin by transferring your design to the fabric using your preferred method (page 16). Once it has been transferred and the fabric is attached to the hoop, start filling in the layers of the mountains. Begin with the top layer and work your way down. Use all 6 strands of each color listed below with a size 5 needle from the DMC Darners Needle pack sizes 1–5. Use satin stitch (page 20) to complete each layer of the hills. The colors for each layer from top to bottom are #3826, #3778, #729, #781 and #3771.

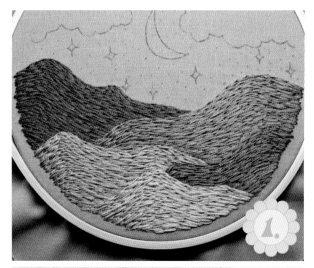

2. Next, switching to an embroidery needle, use DMC Diamant thread in Light Gold and satin stitch to fill in the stars and the moon (see pages 23 and 26 for my Moon and Star Techniques). Use running stitch (page 22) for the tiny dots among the stars.

3. Finally, it's time to add in the clouds! For this, use the size 18 darner needle from the size 14–18 pack. Using the yarn, fill in the clouds with French knots (page 21). Use the Fluffy Cloud Technique (page 24)! Once the clouds are complete, you are done with this beautiful warm-toned landscape. Close the back of the hoop according to the directions on page 27.

warm desert template

ocean at sunset

I don't know if I'm allowed to say this, but this is one of my favorite designs in the entire book! It is just so different than others I have done in the past. The movement of the waves, the French knots—it all ties together so beautifully. It really does have a whimsical feel, and I hope you enjoy stitching it! I would say this design is a bit more advanced as it involves a lot of satin stitching, but this is a one-of-a-kind design that you'll be able to hang proudly on your wall or even give as a gift to an ocean lover!

SUPPLIES NEEDED

Quilting cotton in a light peach, such as Kona cotton fabric in Ice Peach

1 (5-inch [13-cm]) embroidery hoop

1 size 5 darner needle from the DMC Darners Needle pack sizes 1–5

1 embroidery needle

DMC Thread colors: #977, #503, #504, Ecru, DMC Diamant thread in Light Gold

#977   #503   #504   Ecru

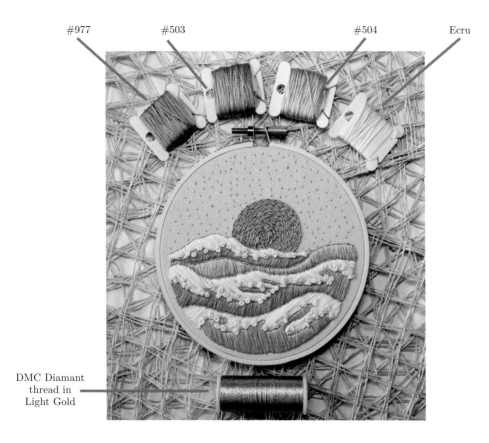

DMC Diamant thread in Light Gold

1. Start by preparing the hoop for stitching and transferring the design on page 83 to the fabric using your preferred method (page 16). Begin by stitching the sun setting over the ocean. Use all 6 strands of #977 and back split stitch (page 19) to complete this. Because you're using all 6 strands, use the size 5 darner needle. This will make stitching with all 6 strands much easier! Start by stitching the outer circle shape of the sun, and slowly stitch that same circular shape along the inside perimeter until you get to the center of the sun. You want the sun to resemble a large spiral.

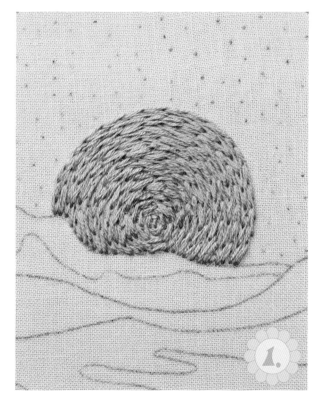

2. Next, let's start stitching the three waves. Leave the wave spray (the twisty white top part of the waves) for last. Stitch the underside of the waves. The first wave, which is the top wave, has two undersides to it. To stitch the part directly under the wave spray, use 6 strands of #503 and satin stitch (page 20). Stitch at a slight angle down and to the left. Use the same technique for the underside of the second wave as well.

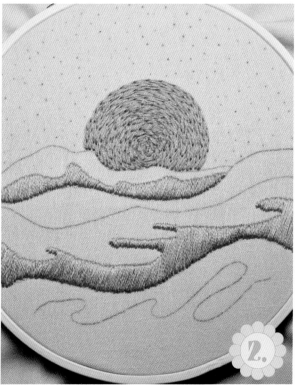

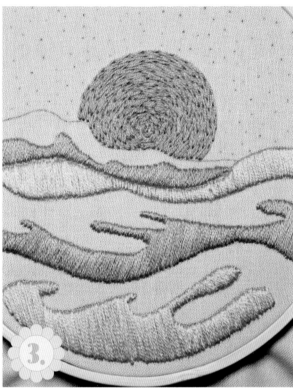

3. Now we will stitch the second part of the first wave, as well as the underside of the very last wave. Use 6 strands of #504 and satin stitch to do this. Stitch at a slight angle pointing down and to the right.

4. It's now time to give these waves some spray! Use 6 strands of Ecru and satin stitch. For the top and middle wave, stitch at an angle down and to the right. For the last wave, stitch at a slight angle down and to the left.

(continued)

5. Next, switch to a regular embroidery needle. Take DMC Diamant thread in Light Gold and use back split stitch to outline the top of the wave sprays and the bottom of the waves. Do not stitch the underside of the wave sprays, though! Also, use the same gold thread and a running stitch (page 22) to add the tiny stars in the sky!

6. Now take 4 strands of Ecru and add some French knots (page 21) in among the wave spray. You can still use a regular embroidery needle to add these French knots. Place these sporadically along the tips of each wave spray, making each wave unique to you! Close off the back of the hoop according to the directions on page 27.

ocean at sunset template

far-out florals & star-speckled skies

Florals in embroidery . . . I know it isn't a surprise! In this chapter, however, I've included some patterns that might feel classic but still exude that same retro theme found throughout this book. Sometimes having a hoop that feels a little more classic, such as Golden Monochrome Flowers (page 105), next to one that is more abstract, such as Starry-Eyed (page 91), provides a nice contrast. Or, stitch a timeless design such as Heart of Gold (page 87) and place it beside any one of The Retro Girls (page 29) to provide a nice complement to one another!

All of this isn't to say that these pieces aren't gorgeous on their own! For instance, Kind Is Cool (page 111) is a fantastic pattern if you want that extra boost of positivity hanging on your wall each day. Just as clothing embroidery was popular throughout the '70s, it would also look amazing stitched on a jacket or shirt. Overall, here you will find designs that contain my spin on floral and abstract art. Just like art from the '70s, in this chapter you will find warm tones mixed with nature themes. My hope is that as you stitch these patterns, the kaleidoscope of colors and contrasts will stir the imagination and ignite the senses.

heart of gold

This is a great beginner pattern to learn how to stitch all the stars found in most of my patterns. Recreating these little retro stars is really a simple process but adds such a powerful punch to a design. Follow these steps and create your very own starry heart hoop! This design is a great complement to the other designs in the book, such as the Kind is Cool (page 111) pattern, for that extra boost of love! This hoop would make such a nice gift for a loved one. Once you get the hang of stitching the stars, you'll finish this hoop in no time!

SUPPLIES NEEDED

Quilting cotton in a light peach, such as Kona fabric in Ice Peach

1 (6-inch [15-cm]) embroidery hoop

1 embroidery needle

DMC Thread colors: DMC Diamant thread in Light Gold, #781, #3776

#781

DMC Diamant thread in Light Gold

#3776

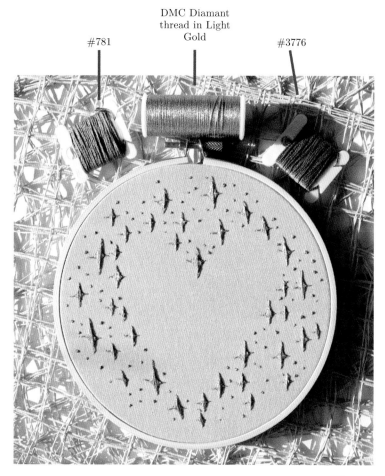

1. Begin by transferring the design on page 90 to your fabric using your preferred method (page 16) and attach the fabric to the hoop. We are going to fill in all the stars first! The first step to creating the star is to stitch basically a lowercase letter "t." Begin by threading your embroidery needle with DMC Diamant thread in Light Gold. Then, pick a star you want to begin stitching. Your first stitch is going to be the small horizontal line. Push your needle up through the underside of the right side of the star and push it down through the fabric on the left side of the star.

2. Now that your small horizontal line is complete, your next step is to stitch the longer vertical line going down the center of the star. To do this, push your needle up through the top point of the star and down through the bottom-middle point of the star.

3. Now you're going to use satin stitch (page 20) to fill in either side of the longer vertical line you just created. These lines should gradually decrease in size when going towards the outer point of the star.

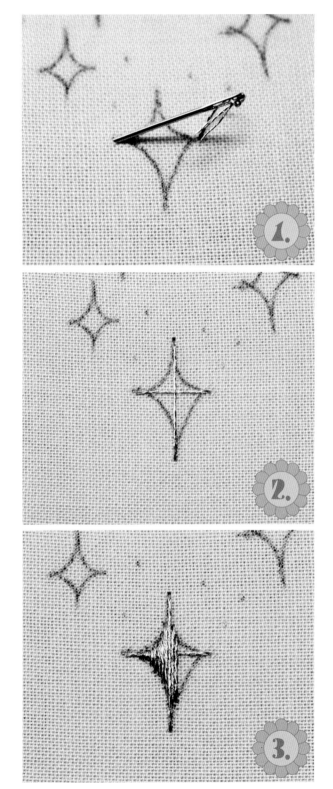

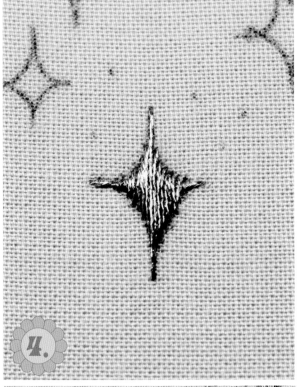

4. The final product should look something like this! A little retro star—crisp and defined.

5. The next step is to stitch all the little dots mixed in between the gold stars. To do this, we are going to use two different colors of thread: 6 strands of #781 and 3 strands of #3776. Use each color to sporadically stitch the little dots using running stitch (page 22). This is a chance to personalize the hoop to your specific taste and choose where you want the little bits of color! Once you've completed this, finish the back of the hoop according to the directions on page 27.

things to note: *This hoop is stitched using my Star Technique. This is a good design to practice the technique on and build up your skills. You can always review more detailed information about my method for stitching stars on page 26. It follows a nearly identical process to what is explained here.*

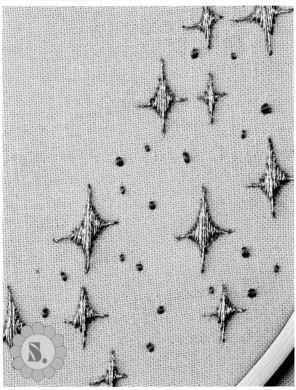

starry-eyed

This design is so unique. I really wanted to create a pattern that was abstract, pretty and could be easily customized to whatever eye color you want! Eyes have always been so fascinating to me. Some say they are the window to the soul, and I think these eyes are no exception. Are these tears of happiness and overwhelming joy or are they from sadness? I think that it can be left up to your imagination!

SUPPLIES NEEDED

Quilting cotton fabric in a creamy white shade

1 (6-inch [15-cm]) embroidery hoop

1 embroidery needle

DMC Thread colors: #310, #935, #732, #780, DMC Diamant thread in Light Gold

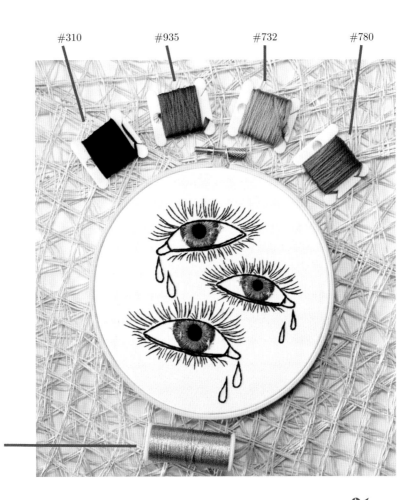

#310   #935   #732   #780

DMC Diamant thread in Light Gold

1. Begin by transferring the design on page 97 to your fabric using your preferred method (page 16) and attaching the fabric to the hoop. Using 3 strands of #310 and back split stitch (page 19), begin to outline the eyes. Start at the inner eye and work your way around to the other side.

2. Next, using 3 strands of #310 and back split stitch, complete the inner rim of the eyes, starting at the outer corner and working your way inward, finishing with the tear duct.

3. Now that the eyes are outlined, let's begin to stitch the eyelashes using back split stitch. To do this, we are going to use a single strand of #310. Start stitching at the base of the eyelashes and work your way to the tip of the eyelash.

(continued)

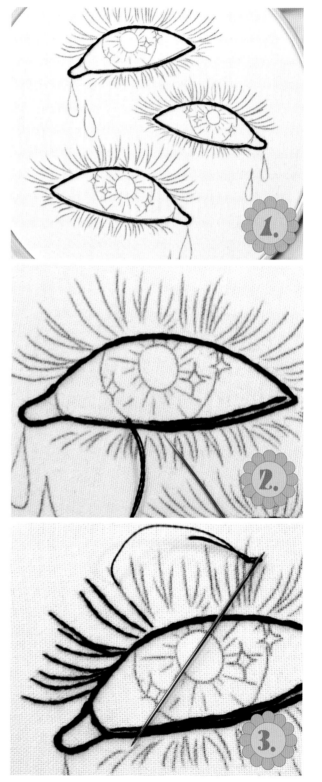

STARRY-EYED (CONTINUED)

4. Next, we are going to start filling in the iris. Take 2 strands of #935 and start stitching the outer rim of the iris, using back split stitch.

5. Once the outer rim is outlined, start adding little stitches pointing in and towards the pupil area using satin stitch (page 20). These little lines should be about ⅓ to ¾ inch (1 to 2 cm) long. Don't worry about making this look perfect, as the next color will blend into this one. These little lines should be placed close together, almost touching.

6. Now we are going to take 2 strands of #732 and repeat the same process, except this time we are going to blend the #732 into the small lines of the #935 that we just stitched. Blending them in to one another will be like completing a back split stitch.

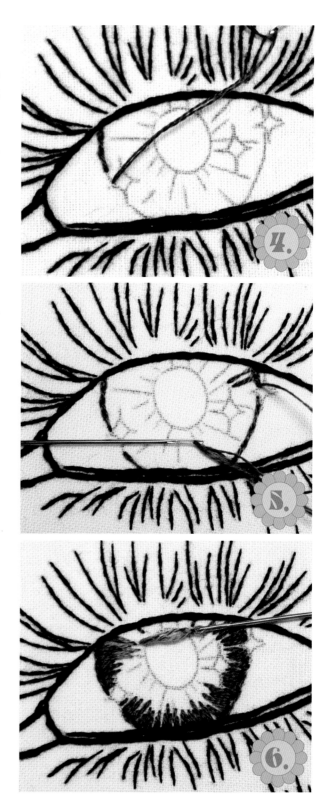

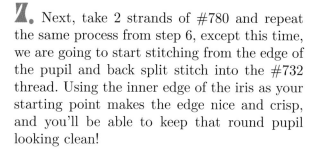

7. Next, take 2 strands of #780 and repeat the same process from step 6, except this time, we are going to start stitching from the edge of the pupil and back split stitch into the #732 thread. Using the inner edge of the iris as your starting point makes the edge nice and crisp, and you'll be able to keep that round pupil looking clean!

8. Now let's fill in the pupil. Taking 2 strands of #310, begin outlining the circle of the pupil using back split stitch. Next, use satin stitch in vertical lines to fill it in. Start at the left side of the pupil and work your way to the right side.

(continued)

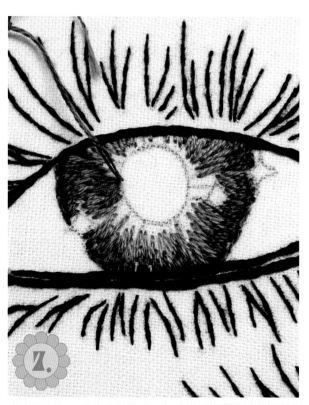

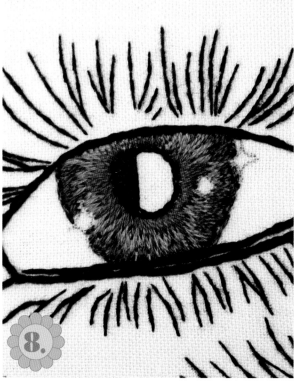

STARRY-EYED (CONTINUED)

9. Star time! Using DMC Diamant thread in Light Gold, use the Star Technique (page 26) to complete the little stars within the eyes.

10. Finally, let's add the tears. To do this, outline the tears using 2 strands of #310 and back split stitch. Yay! You've now finished this hoop. Complete the back of the hoop according to the directions on page 27.

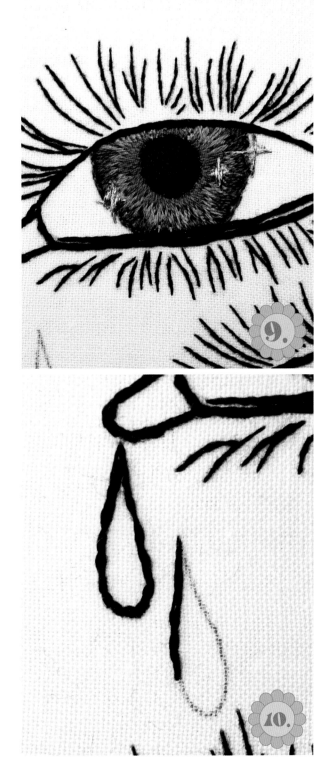

starry-eyed template

moon garden

There's just something about stitching a design on black fabric! The thread colors stand out so nicely and truly pop against the dark tone. Add in a metallic gold moon and gold outlining and it's a recipe for a showstopper! This piece truly reminds me of some of the bold, beautiful fabric patterns and art pieces of the '70s. The pops of color against the dark fabric send a subconscious message of positivity. For this design, I was inspired by the thought of a secret garden at nighttime. In my mind, I envisioned a beautiful garden where the moonlight dances among the flowers and butterflies. This piece would make a fantastic gift for a loved one! So much time and attention to detail is needed for this design, but the result is truly worth it. This whimsical piece will stand out on your wall or shelf and be a conversation starter!

SUPPLIES NEEDED

Quilting cotton fabric in black

1 (6-inch [15-cm]) embroidery hoop

1 embroidery needle

1 size 5 darner needle from the DMC Darners Needle pack sizes 1–5

DMC Thread colors: #21, #3859, #3773, #781, #977, #3856, DMC Diamant thread in Light Gold

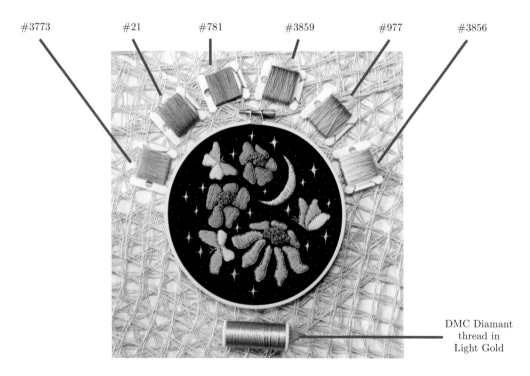

#3773 #21 #781 #3859 #977 #3856

DMC Diamant thread in Light Gold

1. Begin by transferring your design on page 104 to the fabric using your preferred method (page 16) and attaching the fabric to the hoop. We are going to start by stitching the flowers! Using your embroidery needle, 3 strands of #21 and satin stitch (page 20), start with the top center flower. When using satin stitch, stitch in horizontal lines on each petal, following the direction of the petal. Begin your stitches in the inside of the petal and work your way to the outer edges.

2. The next flower that we are going to stitch is the middle flower. Again, using satin stitch and shade #3859, fill in the flower. Use the same technique of working in horizontal lines toward the outer edge of the petal.

3. The last flower we will stitch is the bottom flower. Use #3773 and satin stitch to fill it in. Even though the petals are longer, use the same satin stitch technique to fill them in.

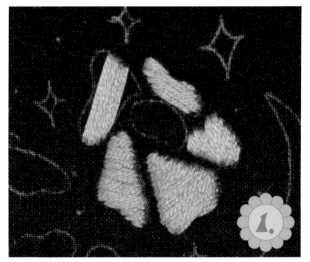

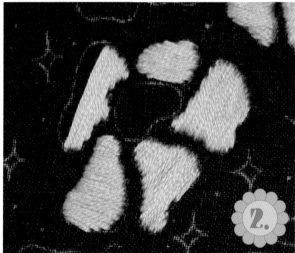

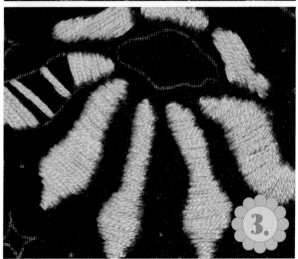

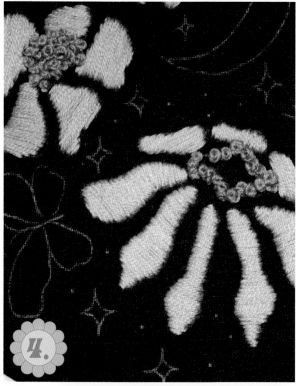

4. Now we need to fill in the center of the flowers. For all three flowers, use 6 strands of #781 and French knots (page 21) to fill it in. Since we are now using all 6 strands of thread, switch to using the size 5 darner needle. The texture of this stitch will really make the flowers pop!

5. Next, let's move on to stitching the butterflies. All three of the butterflies will be stitched with the same technique and colors. Let's begin with the top butterfly. Switching back to your embroidery needle, use 3 strands of #977 and satin stitch to fill in the top wings, and 3 strands of #3856 and satin stitch to fill in the bottom wings. Stitch parallel to the outer slant direction of the wing. Use the same stitching technique for the bottom wings as well.

(continued)

6. Now we need to stitch the body and antenna of the butterflies! To do this, use DMC Diamant thread in Light Gold and back split stitch (page 19). Start by outlining the portions of the wing you've just stitched. Once all the wings are outlined, use the same gold thread and back split stitch to outline the body and antennae.

7. Using the same DMC Diamant thread in Light Gold, use back split stitch to outline the petals of each flower. By having all these outlined, when complete it will look like the moon is reflecting on all the butterflies as well as the flowers!

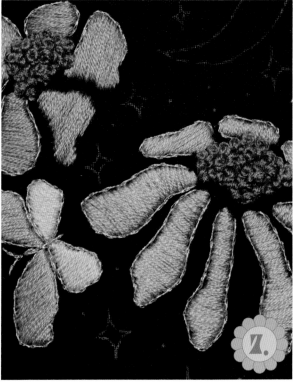

8. Now we've come to the part where we stitch the moon and twinkling stars! Using DMC Diamant thread in Light Gold, use satin stitch to complete these elements. See pages 23 and 26 for more on my Moon and Star Techniques.

9. The last step is to add tiny dots of stars all throughout the hoop. Using DMC Diamant thread in Light Gold, use a running stitch (page 22) to add your own little dots of stars. This will be unique to you and your hoop and will add your finishing touch! Finally, finish the back of the hoop according to the directions on page 27.

moon garden template

golden monochrome flowers

When I started my embroidery journey years ago, monochrome designs were some of the very first types that I loved to create. I love that in a monochrome design, the focus is drawn to the design itself without the busyness of assorted colors competing for attention. A monochrome hoop can be a great addition to a gallery wall because it adds one solid color to the mix and really draws the eye in. I hope you enjoy stitching this fun pattern that feels classic and familiar but with an edgy, modern twist!

 SUPPLIES NEEDED

Quilting cotton in gold or yellow, such as Kona fabric in Curry

1 (6-inch [15-cm]) embroidery hoop

1 embroidery needle

1 size 5 darner needle from the DMC Darners Needle Pack sizes 1–5

DMC Thread color: #3852

#3852 ———

1. Begin by transferring your design on page 109 to the fabric using your preferred method (page 16) and attaching the fabric to the hoop. I've chosen Kona Curry as my fabric of choice. The main thread color I've chosen is #3852, which is a great match for the fabric! We're going to start by stitching the larger flowers. With your regular embroidery needle and 3 strands of thread, use satin stitch (page 20) to fill these in. Work in diagonal lines up each petal pointing towards the center of the flower. For the center of the flower, you are going to use 3 strands of thread and satin stitch again, working in diagonal lines.

2. The next step will be to stitch the branch of leaves. Using 3 strands of #3852 and back split stitch (page 19), trace the outline of the leaves and main branch going down the center.

(continued)

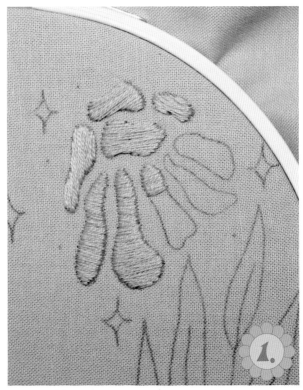

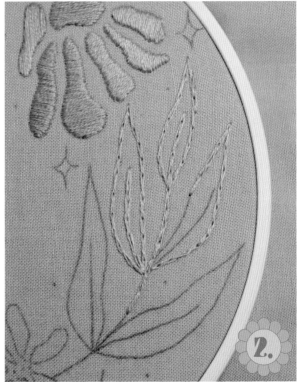

GOLDEN MONOCHROME FLOWERS (CONTINUED)

3. Now we're going to stitch the smaller flowers. Using 6 strands of thread and switching to your darner needle, again use satin stitch in diagonal lines working up toward the center of the flower. We will fill in the center of the flower with French knots (page 21). The thicker petals and the French knots in the center of the flower will give nice dimension and texture!

4. Finally, it's time to fill in the little stars and dots throughout the hoop. Switch back to your embroidery needle and use 3 strands of #3852 and satin stitch to fill in the stars (see page 26 for more on my Star Technique). To complete the little round dots, use 3 strands and French knots. The French knots scattered throughout the design of the hoop will add some visual interest and texture! You've now completed this design. Finish the back of your hoop according to the directions on page 27.

golden monochrome flowers template

kind is cool

This design just gives off good vibes, wouldn't you agree? It displays a heartfelt message. We all need more kindness in our world today! Not to mention, the colors in this hoop are muted and feel calming to the eye. The perfect burnt sienna color of the fabric reminds me of a vintage leather jacket that you might find at the thrift store. This hoop is such a fun project and provides a perfect complement to any of The Retro Girls designs (page 29).

 SUPPLIES NEEDED

Quilting cotton in burnt sienna, such as Kona fabric in Cedar

1 (8-inch [20-cm]) embroidery hoop

1 embroidery needle

1 darner needle from the DMC Darners Needle pack sizes 1–5

DMC Thread colors: #3770, #3820, #3856, #976, #402, #353, DMC Diamant thread in Light Gold

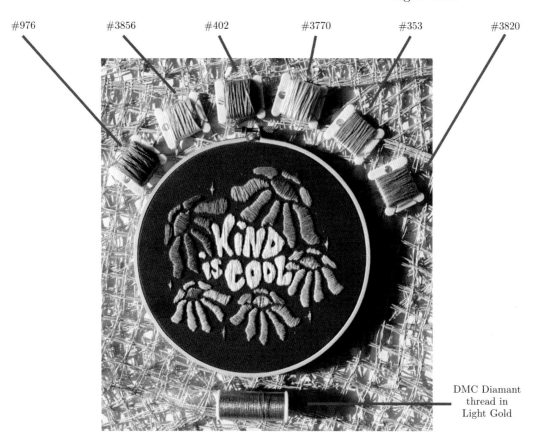

#976 #3856 #402 #3770 #353 #3820

DMC Diamant thread in Light Gold

1. Transfer the design on page 115 to your fabric using your preferred method (page 16) and attach the fabric to your hoop. Let's begin stitching by filling in the words! To start, grab 3 strands of #3770 with your embroidery needle and fill in the words using satin stitch (page 20). Be sure to stitch in vertical lines. These words are the focus of the hoop and will really stand out.

2. Next, let's start filling in the flowers. We are going to work clockwise, starting at the flower in the bottom middle of the hoop. Using all 6 strands of #3820 and switching to your darner needle, begin using satin stitch to fill in the flower, working in horizontal lines. The only exception will be the top middle petal, which is stitched using small vertical lines. Using a darner needle will make it easier to pull all 6 strands of thread through the fabric.

3. Next, we are going to stitch the flower to the left of the yellow flower that we just completed. This time, we are going to grab all 6 strands of #3856. Repeat the same process as step 2 and fill the flower in.

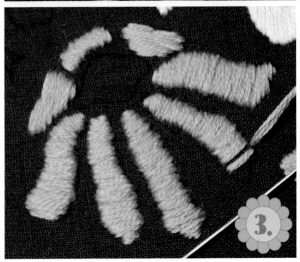

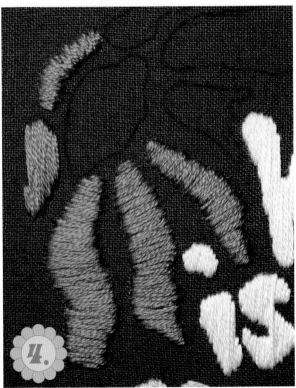

4. Now we are going to stitch the next larger flower above the one we just stitched! Using 6 strands of #976, we are going to repeat the same process as step 2. Continue to work in horizontal lines for each petal, except for the small petal in the top middle of each flower, which will be stitched using vertical lines. Follow this same method of stitching for the rest of the flowers.

5. The next flower going clockwise will also be stitched using satin stitch. Using 6 strands of #402, we are going to fill in the petals of this flower!

(continued)

6. Finally, we've arrived at the last flower! We are going to use #353. This soft baby pink is such a nice complementary color to the rust and mustard tones! Again, use all 6 strands of thread and satin stitch to complete this flower.

7. Now that we have completed the flowers, it's time to fill in the centers of each one. To do this, we are going to use DMC Diamant thread in Light Gold. Switch back to a regular embroidery needle for these. We are also going to use satin stitch, working in vertical lines. I like to start at the left side and work my way right. We are also going to use satin stitch to fill in the little stars (see page 26 for my Star Technique). Satin stitching with metallic thread can be challenging, but take your time. The end result is worth it, I promise! For the stars that are tiny dots, add them in sporadically using running stitch (page 22). Once this step is complete, you can finish the back of the hoop according to the directions on page 27.

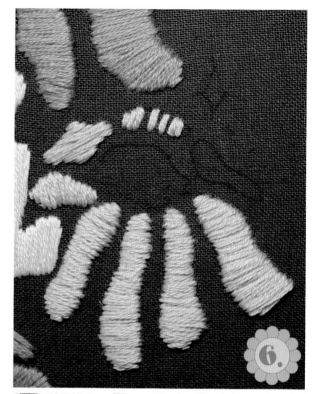

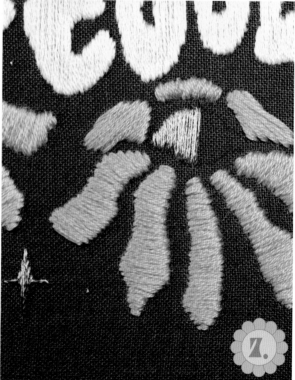

feminine power

Where to begin with these patterns? This chapter contains some of my favorite patterns ever. My goal with these designs was to try and capture the power of women and their attributes. For instance, Girl Power (page 119) is an ode to the kindness and support women show one another. Doesn't the very term "Girl Power" also remind you of the '70s when women were fighting to be seen and heard? Or take, for example, Blooming from Within (page 122), which I made to convey the magic that people hold when bringing a new life into this world.

As women, we carry a storehouse of emotions within us. Gold Dust Woman (page 133) was my first attempt at creating a design within the shape of a woman. When I posted the original design to my Instagram, I couldn't believe how many people sent me messages saying that they could relate to its message of empowerment. Imagine how I felt when one person even messaged me, letting me know they had it tattooed on their body! Overall, I hope when you browse through these images and pick one to stitch for yourself, you're reminded that you are beautiful, capable and worthy of all good things.

girl power

This design was really born out of my love and admiration for the embroidery community that I'm a part of. Witnessing the continuous support and encouragement between artists never fails to amaze me and warm my heart. To find such a loving community—especially during a pandemic—has truly been a blessing. When women stick together, support each other and cheer each other on, we are powerful! I hope you enjoy stitching this fun hoop with a retro twist.

✦ SUPPLIES NEEDED

Quilting cotton fabric in a soft baby pink

1 (8-inch [20-cm]) embroidery hoop

1 embroidery needle

1 size 5 darner needle from the DMC Darners Needle pack sizes 1–5

DMC Thread colors: #310, #3778, #3826, #729, #3771, DMC Diamant thread in Light Gold

#310 #3778 #3771 #3826 #729

DMC Diamant thread in Light Gold

1. Transfer the pattern to the fabric using your preferred method (page 16) and affix the fabric in the hoop. Start by outlining the hands. Use an embroidery needle, 3 strands of #310 and back split stitch (page 19).

2. Next, use satin stitch (page 20) to complete the letters, stitching in vertical lines. Using 6 strands in each of the colors listed, fill in each of the letters. Switch to using the darner needle when stitching these letters. Making each letter a different color adds nice visual interest to the hoop. For the word GIRL (from left to right): #3778, #3826, #729, #3771. For the word POWER (from left to right): #3771, #3778, #3826, #729, #3771.

3. Lastly, switch back to the embroidery needle and use DMC Diamant thread in Light Gold and satin stitch to fill in the stars (see page 26 for more on my Star Technique). Use a running stitch (page 22) to add in the little dots surrounding the stars! Close off the back of the hoop according to the directions on page 27.

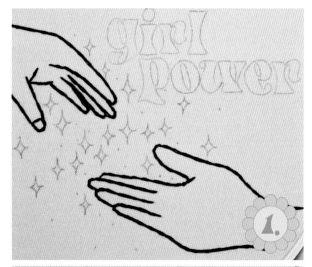

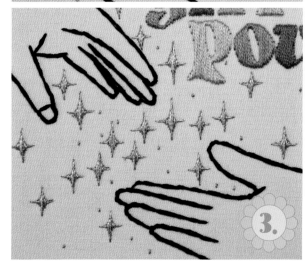

blooming from within

During the writing of this book, I realized one of my dreams when I found out I was pregnant with my second child. This design was created out of the pure joy and love I feel. I very much wanted to encapsulate this moment and how thankful I am. I hope that any other past, current or future pregnant mamas out there can relate to these feelings that come from growing life within you. The flowers are blooming and growing, and the metallic stars add that touch of magic that we feel when carrying life within us.

✦ SUPPLIES NEEDED

Quilting cotton in an amber color, such as Kona fabric in Amber Gold

1 (8-inch [20-cm]) embroidery hoop

1 embroidery needle

1 size 5 darner needle from the DMC Darners Needle pack sizes 1–5

DMC Thread colors: #3371, #832, #3771, #3776, #3852, #3778, DMC Diamant thread in Light Gold

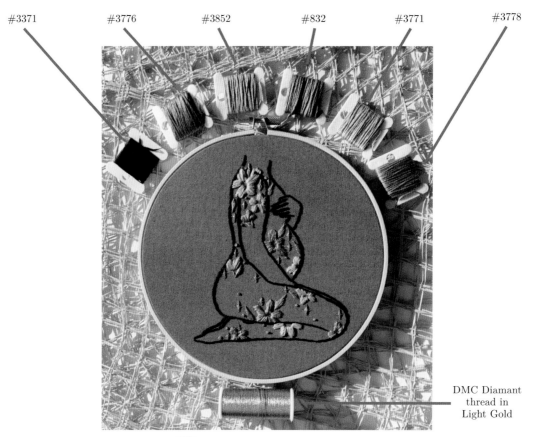

#3371 #3776 #3852 #832 #3771 #3778

DMC Diamant thread in Light Gold

1. Begin by transferring your design on page 127 to the fabric with your preferred method (page 16) and attaching your fabric to the hoop. Next, begin to outline the body of the woman. To do this, use your embroidery needle, 4 strands of #3371 and back split stitch (page 19). Outline all the edges of the woman's body.

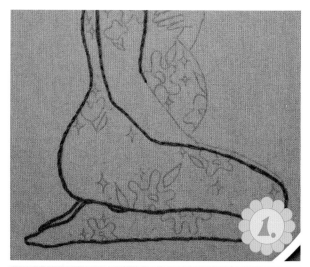

2. Let's start to fill in the foliage by stitching all the leaves. To do this, use 3 strands of #832. Use satin stitch (page 20) for the leaves themselves, and back split stitch for any stems that are attached to the leaves. For the leaves, stitch in vertical lines that point to the tip of the leaf.

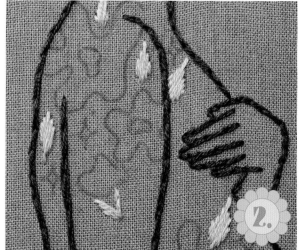

3. Now we'll start to stitch the flowers. We'll start at the shoulders. For the flower at the top of the shoulder, switch to using a darner needle, 6 strands of #3771 and satin stitch to fill it in. Stitch in vertical lines in a clockwise pattern that follows the inner shape of the flower. (We'll use this same technique for all the flowers on the body.) Continue stitching the flower on the lower belly and the middle of the bottom leg.

4. For the next set of flowers, use 6 strands of #3776 and satin stitch to fill in the flower on the middle of the stomach, the kneecap and on the ankle.

5. Next, let's use 6 strands of #3852 and satin stitch to fill in the flower on the right side of the arm, on the lower back and on the top of the thigh. Use the same stitching technique from step 3 for this set of flowers.

(continued)

BLOOMING FROM WITHIN (CONTINUED)

6. Finally, fill in the last two remaining flowers—the flower on the arm and the flower on the bottom of the thigh—using 6 strands of #3778 and satin stitch.

7. Lastly, it's time to add in some gold sparkle of course! Switch to an embroidery needle and, using DMC Diamant thread in Light Gold, fill in the stars and tiny dots of stars. For the larger stars, use satin stitch (see page 26 for more on my Star Technique). For the tiny dots, use French knots (page 21). Once this is complete, and you've finished the back of the hoop (page 27), your beautiful design is done.

blooming from within template

more self-love

I feel like this design has such a good reminder for all of us. For a lot of my life, I've struggled with my body image and have found it hard to feel good about myself at times. This hoop is such a gentle, sweet motto to hang on the wall and look at daily. We need to practice more self-love and be kinder to ourselves! When we are able to do this, I feel like we unlock our confidence and power—and who doesn't want that? This design features butterflies, which can symbolize transformation or joy. This is a great parallel to the '70s, an era when women began to transform and discover they had their own wings to fly. I hope you enjoy stitching this hoop!

✦ SUPPLIES NEEDED

Quilting cotton in a light peach color, such as Kona fabric in Ice Peach

1 (8-inch [20-cm]) embroidery hoop

1 size 5 darner needle from the DMC Darners Needle pack in sizes 1–5

1 embroidery needle

DMC Thread colors: #3826, #781, #3064, #829, #838, DMC Diamant thread in Light Gold

#3064   #829   #3826   #781   #838

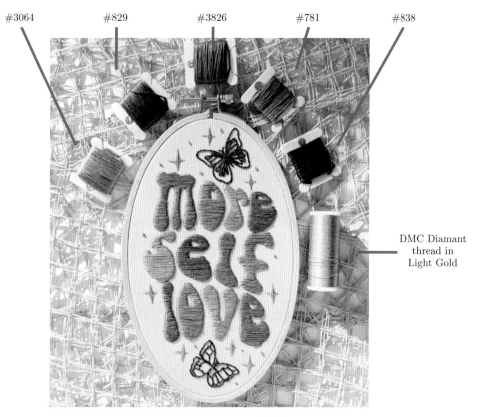

DMC Diamant thread in Light Gold

1. Begin by transferring your design on page 132 to the fabric using your preferred method (page 16) and attaching your fabric in the hoop. We are going to start by stitching the words on this design. Start with the word MORE. From left to right, use colors #3826, #781, #3064 and #829 for each letter. Use 6 strands and satin stitch (page 20) to fill in each letter, stitching in horizontal lines with the darner needle.

2. The next step will be to stitch the word SELF. From left to right, use #3064, #829, #3826 and then #781. Again, use all 6 strands and satin stitch to fill this in.

3. The last word to fill in is LOVE, and again we will use 6 strands of thread and satin stitch for each letter. From left to right, use #829, #781, #3064 and #3826.

4. Now all the words have been filled in and are complete. Let's move on to stitching the two butterflies on the top and bottom of the design. To outline these, use 3 strands of #838 and back split stitch (page 19). Switch to using a regular embroidery needle now. Follow the lines of the butterflies' bodies and wings. When it comes to the antennae, switch to using one single strand of #838 and back split stitch.

5. The next step is adding the tiny gold dots and stars! Use DMC Diamant thread in Light Gold to fill them in. Use satin stitch for the bigger stars (read more about my Star Technique on page 26) and French knots (page 21) for the tiny dots. This will add some nice texture to the design. Once this is complete, your hoop is done! Finish the back of the hoop using the method on page 27.

gold dust woman

The Gold Dust Woman concept came to me one day while I was thinking about the depth of women. We are strong, we are resilient, we adapt to the ever-changing environment that surrounds us. Yet, we are soft like sand, we have smooth edges and hearts of gold that shine brighter than the moon and sun combined. This design remains one of my all-time favorite creations. It's a great intermediate project, especially for practicing satin stitch. By the time the project is complete, you'll be a pro! The warm tones are so comforting and will draw the eye in once it hangs on your wall. I hope you enjoy stitching it for yourself.

SUPPLIES NEEDED

Quilting cotton in a dusty rose color, such as Kona fabric in Rose

1 (5-inch [13-cm]) embroidery hoop

1 embroidery needle

DMC thread colors: #938, #3856, #781, #301, #3852, Ecru, DMC Diamant thread in Light Gold

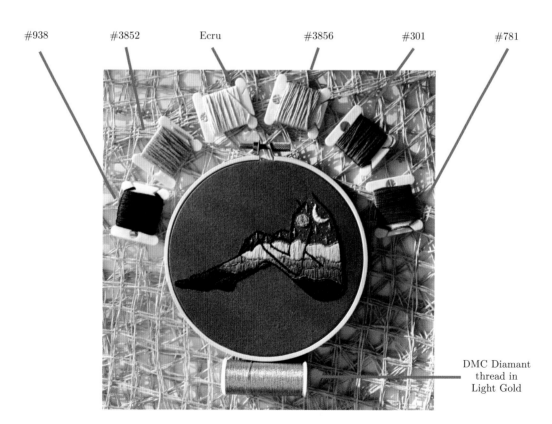

#938 #3852 Ecru #3856 #301 #781

DMC Diamant thread in Light Gold

1. The first step will be to transfer the design on page 138 to your fabric using your preferred method (page 16) and to attach the fabric in the hoop. Begin stitching by outlining the shape of the woman. To complete this, take 3 strands of #938, and using back split stitch (page 19), begin to follow the shape of the woman. I like to start at the neck and down the left side of the body, working my way around to the right side. Use this method to complete the entire outline of the woman, excluding the lines of the desert inside the woman.

2. Let's stitch the desert. We are going to stitch one layer at a time using satin stitch (page 20), working from the top layer to the bottom. To begin, grab #3856 and, using 3 strands, fill in the desert from the left side to the right side, stitching in vertical lines. Repeat this process for the remaining layers of the desert. For the second layer of the desert use #781, for the third layer of the desert use #301 and finally for the fourth layer of the desert use #938.

(continued)

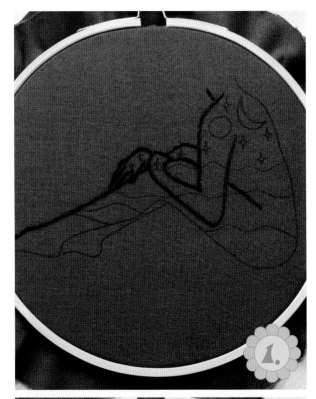

GOLD DUST WOMAN (CONTINUED)

3. Next, we are going to fill in the sky! This is really where the piece starts to come to life. Using 3 strands of #3852 and back split stitch, start by completing the outer circle of the sun and then slowly fill in the sun by following that circular line until you reach the middle. When completed, the sun should look like a tight swirl pattern.

4. Next, we are going to fill in the moon. Grab thread in the shade Ecru, and load the needle using 3 strands. To stitch this, we are going to stitch horizontally and use satin stitch (see page 23 for more on my Moon Technique). Try to follow the curve of the moon while stitching this to give it a bit more of that whimsical look!

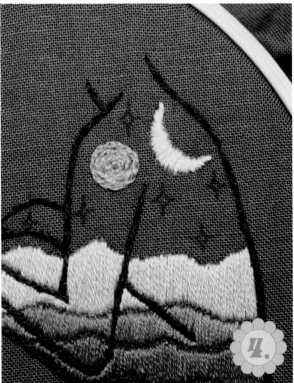

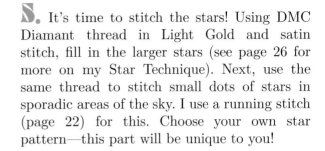

5. It's time to stitch the stars! Using DMC Diamant thread in Light Gold and satin stitch, fill in the larger stars (see page 26 for more on my Star Technique). Next, use the same thread to stitch small dots of stars in sporadic areas of the sky. I use a running stitch (page 22) for this. Choose your own star pattern—this part will be unique to you!

6. It's time to outline the layers of the desert. This will add some beautiful definition and contrast! Using DMC Diamant thread in Light Gold and back split stitch, complete the outlining process. Start with the top layer of the desert, and finish with the bottom. Finish the back of the hoop according to the directions on page 27.

gold dust woman template

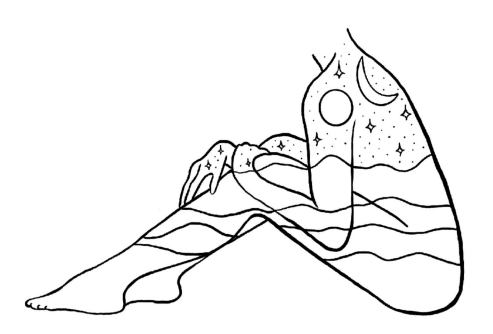

moon river

Although this pattern isn't totally new for me, I knew I had to include it in the book because of how much it has resonated with those who have stitched it. This design is an ode to those quiet moments when you rock your newborn to sleep. When it's the middle of the night, everything else seems to fall away and it's just you and that sweet little baby in your arms in a world of your own. That feeling is what I tried to accomplish with this design. This would be a great gift for a new mom or a mom-to-be! I truly hope you enjoy stitching this!

SUPPLIES NEEDED

Quilting cotton in a soft black

1 (6-inch [15-cm]) embroidery hoop

1 size 5 darner needle from the DMC Darners Needle pack sizes 1–5

1 embroidery needle

DMC Thread colors: #3799, #3064, #3817, #356, DMC Diamant thread in Light Gold

#3799   #3064   #3817   #356

DMC Diamant thread in Light Gold

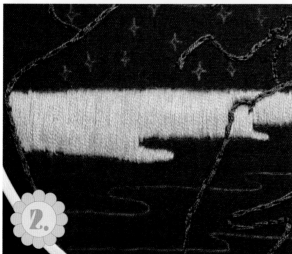

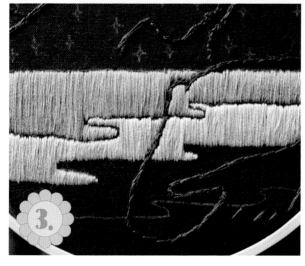

1. Begin by transferring the design on page 144 to your fabric using your preferred method (page 16) and attaching the fabric to the hoop. Once that is done, start by stitching the outline of the mother, baby and the swaddle that the baby is in. Use all 6 strands of #3799 and back split stitch (page 19) to complete this. Using a darner needle will help with pulling all 6 strands through the fabric. Use the darner needle for steps 1 through 4.

2. Next, use 6 strands of #3064 and satin stitch (page 20) to fill in the top layer of the river. Stitch in vertical lines, and stitch from the left side of the river to the right side.

3. The next color we will use is #3817. Using 6 strands and satin stitch, fill in the second layer, again stitching in vertical lines.

(continued)

4. Lastly, fill in the third layer using #356 and satin stitch. Again, use 6 strands of thread to complete this, working in vertical lines.

5. The next step is to use DMC Diamant thread in Light Gold and back split stitch to outline the varying portions of the river. This will add some nice definition and crispness to each layer. Switch to using a regular embroidery needle for steps 5 through 7. Start at the top layer and work your way left to right. Repeat the same process between each layer, finally ending at the bottom of the river.

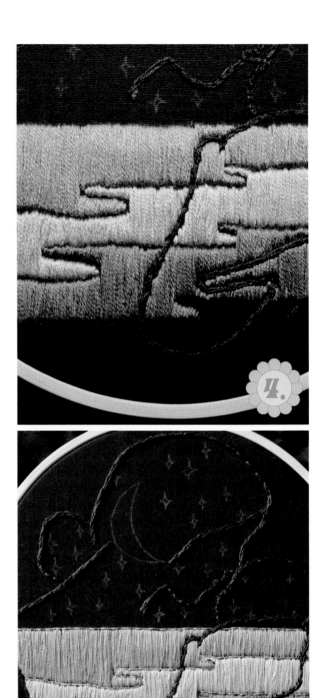

6. Now let's fill in the moon and stars. This adds such a beautiful scope and texture to the sky. Use DMC Diamant thread in Light Gold and satin stitch to complete the moon and larger stars. My techniques for stitching them can be found on pages 23 and 26. For the tiny dots of stars, use a running stitch (page 22).

7. Lastly, let's stitch the little ear on the baby. To do this, use 3 strands of #3799 and back split stitch. Once the little ear is done, so is this hoop! Finish the back of the hoop according to the directions on page 27.

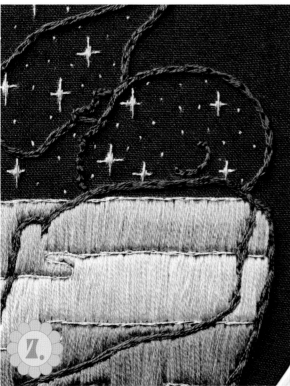

moon river template

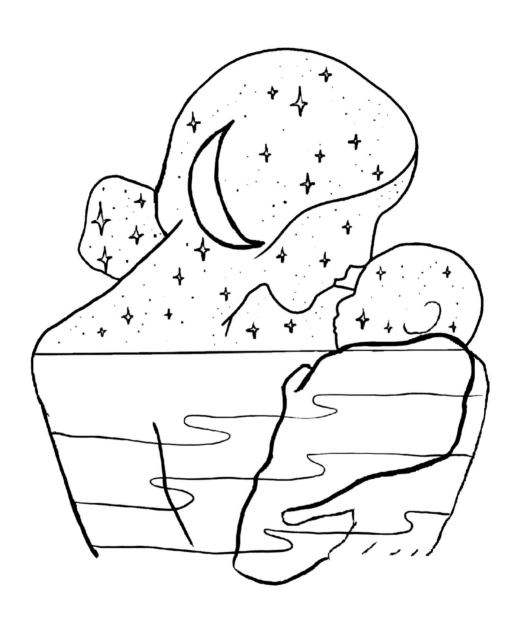

acknowledgments

I could not have written this book without the help of the loving support system that surrounds me.

To my husband, James, thank you for believing in me and nudging me lovingly to take on this challenge. You empower me and love me, which truly made me feel worthy of this opportunity. I love you.

Thank you to my in-laws, firstly Theresa for taking my young son for a few hours every week so I could focus on writing and stitching. I truly could not have done this without your help! Second, thank you Frank for always giving me good advice and encouraging me throughout this process. I am so blessed to have you in my life.

Thank you to my parents for always fostering an environment where I felt like I could be creative and for instilling in me a good work ethic. Thank you to my mom for saving all our art from school, which made me feel loved and like my art was treasured. Thank you to my dad for always encouraging me to be a deep thinker, to become a leader and to have a good sense of humor, which has helped to give me the skills necessary to create and maintain my business. I love you both!

To my sister Erica. Where do I begin? Thank you for giving me some hoops, fabric and thread and encouraging me to start my business. You are my best friend and the creative ideas we bounce off each other and the support you always show me is priceless.

A special thank-you to my followers and community of fellow artists who have always supported me and my art on Instagram. Without your support I could not have had this opportunity. I hope you know the gratitude and appreciation that swells from the bottom of my heart!

Thank you to Page Street Publishing for approaching me to write this book and making my dream come true. Thank you to Franny Donington for being my editor. You were so accommodating and made this process less intimidating than I expected it to be.

Lastly, to my son Elijah and our new little baby on the way. You will always be my proudest creations and my greatest dreams realized. I love you both forever.

about the author

erin essiambre is an embroidery artist living in Nanaimo, British Columbia. She started her business, Salt Water Stitches, in February 2019 as a creative outlet after having her son. In the three years since creating her Instagram account, she has amassed a large, dedicated following and opened a successful Etsy shop. She is best known for her warm color palettes, retro designs and celestial sky hoops. Along with running her business and releasing frequent new designs in her Etsy shop, she is a wife to her husband, James, a full-time stay-at-home mother to her three-year-old son Elijah and growing a new baby on the way!

index